Yvonne Tremblay

THYME IN THE KITCHEN

Cooking with Fresh Herbs

Prentice
Hall
Canada

A Pearson Company
Toronto

Enjoy a fragrant time in your kitchen making these tasty herb dishes!
Yvonne Tremblay

Canadian Cataloguing in Publication Data

Tremblay, Yvonne (Yvonne M.)

Thyme in the kitchen : cooking with fresh herbs

Includes index.

ISBN 0-13-066471-5

1. Cookery (Herbs). I. Title.

TX819.H4T74 2002   641.6'57   C2001-903676-0

ISBN 0-13-066471-5

Editorial Director, Trade Division: Andrea Crozier
Acquisitions Editor: Nicole de Montbrun
Managing Editor: Tracy Bordian
Copy Editor: Kat Mototsune
Proofreader: Marcia Miron
Art Direction: Mary Opper
Cover Design: Mary Opper
Cover Photo: ©FoodPix
Interior Design: Julia Hall
Author Photo: Bryn Gladding Photography
Production Manager: Kathrine Pummell
Page Layout: Gail Ferreira Ng-A-Kien

1 2 3 4 5 WEB 06 05 04 03 02

Printed and bound in Canada.

ATTENTION: CORPORATIONS

Books are available at quantity discounts with bulk
purchase for educational, business, or sales promotional
use. For information, please email or write to: Pearson
PTR Canada, Special Sales, PTR Division, 26 Prince
Andrew Place, Don Mills, Ontario, M3C 2T8. Email
ss.corp@pearsoned.com. Please supply: title of book,
ISBN, quantity, how the book will be used, date needed.

Visit the Pearson PTR Canada Web site! Send us
your comments, browse our catalogues, and more.
www.pearsonptr.ca

Prentice
Hall
Canada

A Pearson Company

To my family,

my parents, Beti and Maurice Tremblay,

and my siblings,

Gerard, Paul, Michelle, Victor and Richard

(who are all great cooks!)

Thank you for all of your support while I follow my dreams.

Contents

Acknowledgments

One thing is certain: you never do these things on your own, especially when you have to pull it all together in six months.

Lise Ferguson, who helped me with my first cookbook in the summer of 2000, enthusiastically agreed to help me with this one. (We both had a touch of amnesia about how much work it was the last time.) Lise input most of the recipes, editing as she went and skillfully filling in the blanks. (Sometimes when you are testing you forget to write down some of the details. Luckily for me, Lise is also an expert cook as well as a copy editor.) Thank you, Lise, for your encouraging talks, the shared laughter and for frequently saying, "Give me that; you don't need to spend time doing that!" We are soul sisters!

A thank-you to my friend Patricia Moynihan-Morris (food consultant), who tested the bread recipes and some of the baking in this book. Pat is a traditional yeast-bread and bread-machine expert who teaches inspiring classes on breads as well as on English teas.

A thank-you to my friend Sonja, whom I met when I was teaching courses on cooking with fresh herbs. Sonja was always there during the creation of this book, offering help, her sunny smile and big hugs. She grew herbs in her garden this summer so I could have extra for testing, picked up groceries (and sometimes dinner), even delivered the final manuscript to the publisher. One day, when I was having a rough go of it, she showed up at the door with a bouquet of herbs and herb flowers in her hand.

Thanks to my friends Sandra, Rose, Luisa, Micki, Wendi, Judy and Heather, who gave me ideas for the kinds of recipes to include in the book, and who kept in touch while I was sequestered on this project.

Thanks to Carol Ferguson, my friend Rose, my mom, my brother Richard, Foodland Ontario and the International Olive Oil Council for contributing recipes.

A thank-you to Bryn Gladding, my friend and professional photographer, who generously took my photo for the back cover on his day off and who also photographed the herbs for the Herb Directory.

I am grateful to the management and my co-workers at Faye Clack Marketing & Communications (where I started a job as food consultant at the same time I started this book!) for all their support and taste testing. Cory gave me extra time off to work on the book in the summer and near the end when I was in the crunch, otherwise I would not have had any sleep at all!

An extra-special thank-you goes to Nicole de Montbrun, Acquisitions Editor at Prentice Hall Canada, who convinced the publisher to bring the book out (and thanks for being flexible with deadlines). I applaud the managers, especially Tracy Bordian, and creative team, whose care and professional touches contributed to these beautiful results. And a thank-you to Kat Mototsune for her astute attention to details in her copy edit.

Finally, thanks to you, reader, for taking this book home with you. I hope it will help you find the joy of growing and using herbs, and open up a world of new and wonderful tastes.

Yvonne Tremblay

Introduction

It is late summer as I am writing this. My herb garden looks incredible after a summer that, while low in rain, was sunny and warm—perfect conditions for abundant leaf production. I have allowed some of the herbs to go to flower and to seed, bringing small bouquets of assorted herbs indoors to enjoy as I create recipes for you.

In the past few years, popular culinary herbs have found their way into produce stores and produce sections of supermarkets, so most fresh herbs are available year-round. You don't even have to grow them yourself! However, if you have a little space and the right conditions, do try it yourself—they are actually quite easy to grow. And it's so handy to have a herb garden just outside your door, so you can cut them fresh and take just what you need. Having your own herb garden also allows you to grow herbs that are not normally found in stores, such as lemon thyme, purple basil, orange mint and many others. A number of herbs are perennial and will return on their own, so you can have an abundant supply every year with minimal effort.

For years I have taught classes on how to cook with fresh herbs. Many of my students tell me that they like to grow herbs but they don't know what to do with them, or that they buy herbs, needing only a small amount for a recipe, and don't know what to do with the rest. With this book I hope to accomplish two goals: first, to help you get full enjoyment out of using fresh herbs to liven up your cooking and eating; and second, to show you how to capture the flavor of fresh herbs for later use. To accomplish this, I will provide you with information on how to grow your own herbs, when to pick them, when to add them to food and how to store them so they will last, and I will introduce you to some great recipes.

Herbs are used in many of the world's cuisines, often giving the signature taste to a dish. Cooking with fresh herbs is a leading-edge trend, really a revival. With a little basic knowledge you can transform your cooking into something exciting, at the same time enjoying some aromatherapy! The recipes in this book are simple and easy to follow. You do not have to be a great cook to master the skill of using fresh herbs, but your results will make people think you are.

It is my belief that, when food tastes really satisfying, we slow down, enjoy each mouthful and do not overeat. Cooking with fresh herbs makes healthier foods—vegetables, fish and legumes—taste great. I sincerely hope that this book will open up a whole new realm of cooking for you as well as bring greater satisfaction to your eating and those you may cook for.

My first cookbook, *Prizewinning Preserves*, was published in 2001. I had barely started that book when I proposed the idea for a herb cookbook to the publishing company. They gave me a wholehearted go-ahead and, as a consequence, I have spent a lot of "thyme" in the kitchen this summer. Next summer it will be time on my sailboat, which I had to ignore this year. But putting together this book is one of my life's dreams and I am very excited to be bringing it to you.

There isn't enough room to include all the recipes I would like to put in this book. I have developed and selected a wide range of recipes as a place for you to start to gain some experience and confidence. You will begin to know what herbs go best with what types of food and what flavors you enjoy most. You can then apply some of the principles to other recipes or create variations of your own.

So, here we go. Your cooking will never be the same!

Basics

Throughout this book, the following assumptions have been made:

- You are using *freshly squeezed* lemon juice, *freshly ground* black pepper, *freshly grated* Parmesan cheese, *extra-virgin* olive oil.

- You are using *large* eggs, *salted* butter.

- Herbs are washed and removed from stems before using.

- Edible flowers are organically grown (pesticide- and herbicide-free).

- Dry measures are used for dry ingredients, including herbs; liquid measures are used for all liquids and are measured at eye level.

Note that metric measurements are equivalents and were not used in development.

Terms

Finely chop: to cut into very small pieces (about 3/16 inch/4 mm)

Mince: to chop in pieces smaller than very finely chopped (1/8 inch/2mm or less)

Dice: to cut evenly into cubes or squares 1/2 inch/1 cm or smaller

Chiffonade: when leaves of herbs such as basil and sage are stacked, rolled lengthwise into a "cigar," then finely sliced into strips or ribbons

Infuse: to steep herbs in a liquid—such as oil, vinegar, water, juice, milk, tea, etc.—to extract the flavor; the result is an infusion.

Useful Equipment

Mortar and pestle; mini-prep food processor; salad spinner; good quality chef's knife; wooden cutting board for savory foods and herbs; plastic cutting board for fruits and sweet herbs (e.g., mint); oven thermometer.

Part 1

A Primer on Herbs

What Are Herbs?

Herbs are plants found primarily in the temperate climates of the northern hemisphere. Specifically, herbs are the leaves of soft green plants and low bushy shrubs, as well as leaves of the bay laurel tree. Botanically, true herbs also include plants that yield dried seeds (i.e., anise, cumin, coriander, dill, fennel, parsley, etc.).

Spices come mainly from tropical regions and are the barks, flower buds, fruit or root bulbs of trees. They are seldom used without first being dried.

In this book I will focus on the most common *culinary* herbs, leaving the medicinal uses of herb plants to other sources.

Using Herbs

Fresh vs. Dried

It is the aromatic (volatile) oils that give fresh herbs their unique flavor. These are concentrated when the herb is dried. The rule of thumb for substituting fresh herbs for dried in recipes is 3 to 1. Use 1 tbsp/15 mL chopped fresh herbs for every 1 tsp/5 mL dried herbs.

Exceptions
Rosemary
Substitute fresh for dried in equal amounts, as it does not diminish in size when dried and has a strong flavor when fresh.

Tarragon
Use half the amount of fresh as dried, as its flavor is more intense when fresh than dried.

How to Measure Fresh Herbs

Fresh herbs are usually chopped before measuring, except when used whole or in pesto. See the "Terms" on page x in the Introduction: finely chopped means cut into small pieces; minced means *very* small pieces; snipped means cut with kitchen scissors (e.g., chives are snipped into 1/2-inch/1 cm lengths.)

Always pack herbs loosely into measuring spoons and cups (unless instructed otherwise). They should be level, not packed. You can always add more to a dish after tasting. Some herbs can be overpowering if used with a heavy hand.

Herb Mixtures

The following terms are commonly referred to in recipes.

Bouquet Garni

French term used to describe a small bunch of fresh herbs. It consists of one bay leaf, a sprig of thyme and several sprigs of parsley, complete with long stalks. The parsley is usually wrapped on the outside of the bunch to prevent the thyme leaves from being knocked off during cooking. The bunch is tied with a piece of kitchen string, with a long strand that is draped over the edge of the pot so it can be easily removed after flavor has been imparted to the food. It is used in stews, ragouts and meat casseroles.

Fines Herbes

French term meaning "finely chopped herbs," it refers to "sweet herbs" consisting of chervil, chives, parsley and tarragon used together in equal amounts. It can also include basil or marjoram. Fines herbes are best with egg dishes, and with food that requires no cooking or light cooking. Delicious in sandwich fillings, cream cheese and green salads such as mesclun mix.

Herbes de Provence

Originating in Provence, France, this is a blend of usually dried herbs (but can be made fresh) that includes thyme, marjoram, rosemary and bay leaves. It occasionally includes summer savory, sage or lavender, and sometimes basil. It has a multitude of uses: as a marinade for grilled chicken, sprinkled on pizza before cooking, in potato soup, with chèvre cheese, roast lamb or pork, with fish, in breads, in honey, etc. Purchase commercially in kitchen stores or try this recipe to make your own. Best if made from fresh dried herbs (see "Drying Herbs," page 17).

Herbes de Provence

1 tbsp	dried thyme leaves	15 mL
1 tbsp	dried marjoram or oregano leaves	15 mL
1 tbsp	dried rosemary leaves	15 mL
1 tbsp	dried summer savory leaves	15 mL
2	dried bay leaves, finely crushed	2
1 tsp	dried lavender flowers, optional	5 mL

1. In a small bowl combine thyme, marjoram, rosemary and savory leaves. Lightly crumble with your fingers. Stir in crushed bay leaves. Add lavender (if using).

2. Store in a covered glass jar in a cool, dark place. Keeps for up to a year.

Tips for Cooking with Herbs

The distinctive flavor of any herb should not be allowed to become too prominent, but should remain tantalizingly in the background. The secret is to know when a little is enough. You can always add a little more if needed.

- Do not use herbs in every dish or course in a meal.
- Do not season more than one dish in the same meal with the same herb.
- Do not fry herbs along with meat or fish, as they end up as bitter, black specks. Herbs for flavoring fried foods should be served in an accompanying sauce or be finely chopped and sprinkled over the dish at the time of serving.
- In general, fresh herbs don't stand up to long cooking, so add right before the dish is done.
- Herbs for casseroles and stews should be added after the liquid has been added to the pre-browned meat.
- Herb salad dressings and cold sauces should be made well ahead of time so that flavors have time to blend thoroughly.
- Chop fresh herbs well to bring out all their flavor and aroma. When using dried herbs, crush them first by rolling them between your hands, or crush with a mortar and pestle. This will release their essential oils.
- Herbs that are "ground" or "powdered" will lose their character more quickly than whole leaves.
- Replace dried herbs as soon as they lose their scent and color, turning pale and grayish, as they will have lost most of their flavor too. If they do not have their own distinctive smell, they are useless in food and may as well be discarded. If you don't know how long you have had your herbs, throw them out and get new ones.
- Store dried herbs away from the light in a cool, dry place to prevent loss of color and flavor. The worst place to store herbs is above the stove. A spice rack or turntable inside a cupboard is a good choice.
- When buying dried herbs, do not buy the cheapest brands in tin containers or from bulk bins. The more expensive brands are often the best in the long run. Always store dried herbs in glass jars with airtight lids.

Herb Directory

Basil (also called sweet basil)

Growing: An annual; grow in full sun; vulnerable to frost

Flavor Profile: Spicy, sweet, anise (licorice) and clove-like; flavor changes when dried. Purple basil (opal, ruffled) has a more delicate flavor that is clove-like. Other varieties include cinnamon basil, lemon basil, Thai basil and globe basil (small leaves, great for drying).

Uses: Salads, soups, dips and sauces, stews, rice dishes; as part of fines herbes mixture; frequent addition to Italian tomato dishes; excellent in red lentil soup, gazpacho, ratatouille. Good in omelettes, egg salad, cottage cheese; main ingredient of pesto (see page 141); great with tomatoes, eggplant, zucchini. Purple basil makes a beautiful red vinegar.

Note: Leaves are very delicate; handle gently; wash and chop just before using.

Bay Leaves (also called laurel leaf)

Growing: A perennial evergreen tree; grow in full sun to partial shade

Flavor Profile: Slightly bitter, savory

Uses: Soups and chowders; add to water for cooking vegetables (i.e., potatoes) or pasta; spaghetti sauce, casseroles, stews; meat, especially beef dishes, chicken and turkey; fish (when poaching shrimp or cooking shellfish); in marinades; part of bouquet garni; in milk to flavor rice pudding. Almost indispensable in cooking.

Note: Seldom used fresh, as dried bay leaves have a better, sweeter flavor than fresh; flavor intensifies the longer it cooks. Remove at end of cooking.

Chervil

Growing: An annual; grow in partial shade; sow from seeds; goes to seed easily, especially if dry; plant every two weeks for steady supply

Flavor Profile: Mild anise-pepper, parsley; delicate fern-like leaves. Two main types: plain and curly

Uses: Poultry and fish dishes (oysters); egg dishes; soups (vichyssoise); with tomatoes, in tartar sauce, as a garnish; part of fines herbes mixture (see page 3). Goes well with any new vegetables, such as new peas, potatoes, baby carrots, asparagus.

Note: This herb is a staple of French cooking, so is often called French parsley. Add at end of cooking to preserve its delicate flavor.

Chives

Growing: A perennial; grow in full sun to partial shade; flowers in June; remove flower stalks as soon as they appear to prevent loss of flavor

Flavor Profile: Onion chives—thin, hollow leaves, mild onion flavor; garlic chives—flat leaves like blades of grass, mild onion/garlic flavor

Uses: Omelettes, quiche, cheese spreads and dips, tuna salad; sprinkled over broiled tomatoes, green salad, potato salad, potato soup, baked potatoes and other vegetables; to garnish soups. The purple flowers of onion chives are edible (soups, salads), have an oniony flavor and make a beautiful pink-purple vinegar.

Note: Use kitchen scissors to snip chives, rather than cutting or chopping them.

Cilantro (also called fresh coriander, Chinese parsley)

Growing: An annual; grow in full sun to partial shade; goes to seed easily; plant every two weeks for steady supply

Flavor Profile: Citrus and sage

Uses: Chicken, fish, lamb and rice, pasta or vegetable dishes. Also good in salsa, taco fillings, black bean and corn salad, lentil or black bean soups; in butters for vegetables or fish. Distinctive flavor found in Caribbean, Indian, Thai, Chinese, Mexican and Latin American dishes. Seems to go well with most "hot" cuisines. Seeds (coriander) also used, can be collected and ground.

Note: Leaves do not retain flavor well when dried.

Dill (also called fresh dill or dillweed)

Growing: An annual; grow in full sun, look for Fern Leaf dill; goes to seed easily

Flavor Profile: Parsley, anise and celery, subtle lemon. Feathery leaves are used.

Uses: Lentil, bean or pea soups; in all egg dishes, with cheese and most fish; lamb, chicken. Add to dressing for sliced cucumbers or with beets. Delicious in potato, tuna, egg or pasta salads, with cabbage, seafood cocktail, salad dressings; dips, sauces for fish. Seeds, which have a stronger flavor, used in breads, salads, pickling.

Note: Name derives from Norse *dilla*, meaning "to lull," as it was used to induce sleep.

Lavender

Growing: An evergreen shrub, perennial in some climates, especially if protected from winter elements; grow in full sun

Flavor Profile: Sweet, sharp, pungent; look for English lavender

Uses: In desserts, sugars, syrups, preserves, vinegars, with fruit such as peaches, raspberries, strawberries, apples

Note: Use only organically grown (without herbicide and pesticides) flowers.

Lemon Balm (also called sweet Melissa)

Growing: A perennial; grow in full sun to partial shade

Flavor Profile: Lemon with hint of mint

Uses: Poultry dishes (or stuffing) and with pork chops; with shrimp, lobster and mussels; with vegetables; in green or fruit salads; to make vinegars. Dried leaves make a pleasant tea or addition to black tea. Add leaves to white wine.

Marjoram (also called sweet marjoram)

Growing: A perennial, but treat like an annual where winter temperatures go below freezing; grow in full sun; distinctive knot-like flower buds

Flavor Profile: Perfumy, subtle lemon with hint of balsam, more delicate than oregano

Uses: Pasta sauces; with veal and pork roasts; with ground beef (meatloaf, shepherd's pie); in scrambled eggs and omelettes; with bread cubes for stuffing; in chicken liver pâté; with green beans, mushrooms, carrots; in lentil, pea, bean, potato soups; when grilling or baking fish. Ideal for lamb; in stews, marinades, herb butters. Common in French, Italian and Portuguese cooking.

Mint

Growing: A perennial; grow in full sun to partial shade; will overtake (plant in pots to contain)

Flavor Profile: Sweet-flavored, cool and refreshing; flavor varies from the heat of peppermint and coolness of spearmint to the fruitiness of apple mint, pineapple mint and orange mint; even chocolate mint

Uses: New potatoes, green beans, tabbouleh salad or with tomatoes as a change from basil; mint sauce or jelly for lamb. Sprinkle chopped fresh mint on top of green pea soup. Put a sprig in the water when boiling green peas or potatoes. Adds a refreshing taste to fruit salads, iced tea and lemonade. Stir into cream cheese spreads; garnish for desserts.

Oregano (also called wild marjoram)

Growing: A perennial; grow in full sun; look for Greek oregano for best flavor

Flavor Profile: Earthy and intense with hints of clove and balsam

Uses: In almost any tomato dish; pasta sauces, pizza, chili con carne, barbecue sauce. Excellent in egg and cheese dishes; meat or poultry stuffings; on pork, lamb, chicken and fish. Essential ingredient of chili powder. Common in Italian, Greek and Mexican dishes.

Note: This herb is best used dried.

Parsley

Growing: A biennial; grow in full sun to partial shade

Flavor Profile: Mild, savory flavor, slightly peppery; curly or Italian (flat leaf) parsley most common types—Italian has a stronger flavor

Uses: In pasta dishes, sauces, scrambled eggs, soups, mashed or boiled potatoes, vegetable dishes (carrots, cabbage, tomatoes, turnip, beets); with poultry or fish. When making soup or stew, add the whole frond and remove before serving. Blends well with other herbs. Part of bouquet garni and fines herbes. Great deep-fried or in tempura batter. Use for garnish, especially sprinkled chopped over stews, pasta dishes and casseroles that need a bit of color.

Note: Dried parsley is a poor substitute for fresh. A quick way to chop parsley leaves is in a glass measuring cup using kitchen scissors. For large quantities, chop in a food processor.

Rosemary

Growing: A perennial in some areas; grow in full sun to partial shade

Flavor Profile: Piney, resinous with hint of lemon; works well with basil or thyme

Uses: Beef, lamb, veal, pork, rabbit, goose, duck and poultry; for roasts, make slits with a knife and insert garlic slivers and rosemary leaves. Rosemary is particularly good with lamb. Use when cooking eggplant, squash and in sauce for lasagna; in vinegars, oils and marinades; with thyme for frying or roasting potatoes, focaccia, marinated olives. In baking cookies, breads, cornbread, biscuits, etc.

Note: When using individual fresh leaves (vs. sprigs), always chop finely, as leaves are tough. Dries well.

Sage

Growing: A perennial; grow in full sun

Flavor Profile: Earthy, musty mint, camphor-like with hint of lemon. English pineapple sage, purple sage and variegated sage are most popular varieties. Combines well with rosemary, thyme or marjoram.

Uses: Stuffings for poultry, fish, game and other meats; in sauces, soups and chowders, meat pies; in marinades; in barbecue sauces with rosemary and thyme. Use sparingly. For roast pork: with a sharp knife, make slits in the skin 1/4 inch (5 mm) apart; brush with olive oil to which a handful of fresh crushed leaves has been added. Excellent deep-fried as an appetizer or garnish, in Saltimbocca (see page 110); in herbal oil to brush over meats, yeast breads. Good with onions, cabbage, carrots, corn, eggplant, squash, tomatoes and other vegetables.

Note: Used in commercial sausage (so-sage!).

Savory

Growing: An annual (summer savory) or perennial (winter savory); grow in full sun

Flavor Profile: Summer savory—aromatic, peppery, more readily found and more subtle in flavor than winter savory; resembles thyme and marjoram. Winter savory—stronger with a more piney flavor.

Uses: With any kind of beans or legumes; with Brussels sprouts, cabbage, corn. Add a sprig to the water when cooking green or wax beans, lima beans or green peas; flavor dressings for bean or potato salad; add a pinch to split-pea soup, lentils. Sprinkle chopped on grilled tomatoes, on sliced cucumbers. Include in stuffings for chicken, turkey or pork. Good with ground lamb; in meatloaf, chicken or beef soups. Mix chopped savory and grated lemon rind with breadcrumbs for a coating for veal or fish. Winter savory is especially good in pâtés and with game meats.

Note: Leaves dry very well and retain flavor, which is less lemony and more musty than fresh.

Tarragon

Growing: A perennial, but may not overwinter in cold areas; grow in full sun to partial shade; difficult to grow from seed, but available as small plants from nurseries in early spring

Flavor Profile: Sweet, anise-like (licorice); look for French tarragon for best flavor

Uses: In soups, fish/shellfish and egg dishes; green salads, French salad dressing. Add tarragon vinegar to tartar sauces served with poached salmon, or to make mayonnaise. Mix with butter and lemon to serve with most grilled fish. Also good with chicken, port, beef, lamb, game; distinctive flavor in Bernaise sauce. Good with green beans, asparagus, peas or carrots. Used widely in French cooking, part of fines herbes mixture.

Thyme

Growing: A perennial; grow in full sun to partial shade

Flavor Profile: Slightly pungent, spicy, savory, clove-like. Lemon thyme—a bit milder, with a lemony flavor. Blends well with other herbs, especially rosemary.

Uses: All meats, vegetables, casseroles, soups, stuffings, meatloaf, marinades and pâtés. Excellent for herb bread and flavored butters. Good with mushrooms, fried potatoes, carrots (and other vegetables) and in omelettes. Commonly used in clam chowder and gumbo; used in French, Creole and Cajun cooking. Lemon thyme is excellent with fish and chicken.

Note: Has a strong flavor, so only a little is needed. Dries well.

Growing Your Own Herbs

Growing your own herb garden can be a rewarding experience. You will always have your favorite herbs on hand and you can cut as much as you need. They will always be fresher than store-bought, too. This is especially beneficial when you are drying them or preserving them in oils, vinegars, butters, etc. You get to pick the best leaves, at their freshest. You have access to the flowers, too, which are not usually included in store-bought herbs (which are picked just before flowering).

Herbs can be grown outdoors in the summer, or indoors in the winter on a windowsill or under fluorescent lights. You can bring some of your outdoor plants indoors for the winter, but be sure to allow a transition period; dig up the plant and place it in a pot with plenty of its own soil and good drainage. Then leave it outside for two weeks until it has adjusted to the potting. For indoor growing, keep soil damp and maintain drainage. Use top-quality potting soil that drains well and is pH balanced. Provide sunlight and fresh air, but avoid drafty areas.

Plant herbs in a small herb bed, tucked in among your flowers or in boxes or pots on a balcony. Most herbs—basil, tarragon, marjoram, rosemary, savory and thyme—thrive in hot sun. Chervil and most mints require shade in summer; parsley and sage do better in partial shade, though they survive strong sun. Anise, coriander, cumin, caraway and dill require sun for ripening the seed.

Growing Herbs in Pots

For growing in pots, terra cotta is best for drainage and air. The size of the pot will determine the size of the herb plant you end up with. Larger pots will result in larger plants with more leaves for harvesting. If the plant is too small, you will have to wait a while for the leaves to grow back before cutting again. A 10-inch (25 cm) diameter pot is a good size.

Plant one variety per pot. Mixed pots of herbs are not recommended, unless they all thrive on the same amount of sun and moisture. Some herbs grow faster and larger than others and may take over the pot. If you have a large window box or container that gives them each plenty of room, they may do well.

Soil
The soil should be free-draining, sandy loam. Avoid soil that is nitrogen rich, as the herb's flavors will not be as strong. Obtain soil from a nursery or mix up your own using equal amounts of soil, river sand (not salty sand) and leaf mold. *Herbs do not like wet feet!* If there is no drainage hole in your container, provide a thickly pebbled drainage bed and regulate watering carefully. Do not use weed killers or pesticides around your herbs.

Outdoor Growing Tips

- Full sun produces the best herbs.
- Fertilizer produces large plants with lush foliage and strong roots. Use time-released synthetic fertilizer or organic fish fertilizer every two to three weeks. Fertilize bedding plants after planting in the ground to help them get established.
- Watering: *Wet Herbs* (basil, chives, dill, lemon balm, mint and parsley) like lots of water. Plant separately from others. *Dry Herbs* (marjoram, oregano, rosemary, sage, thyme) like to dry between waterings. (If they are wilting, then they are too dry!) Feel about 1 inch (2.5 cm) into the soil; if dry at that level, they need watering.
- Regular pruning is the best way to get lush, bushy plants and the new growth often has the best flavor. Trim just above the leaf node (where the leaf emerges from the stem) by pinching the stem with your fingers. Or prune with garden shears about one-third of the way down the stem. Remove any yellowed or damaged leaves.
- Once the plant flowers, the leaves will have less flavor. Regular trims will delay blossom formation. Pinch off developing flower buds (heads) to postpone maturation. I like to let some go to flower at the end of the season. Flower blossoms are edible and taste like the herb they come from, only milder; use in salads or butters, and to decorate herb vinegars.
- Herbs of the *umbellifer* family (coriander, dill, etc.) have a tendency to go to seed more quickly than other herbs (see "Herb Seeds," page 40). You may wish to do successive plantings to ensure a steady supply through the summer.
- Mulching around your plants helps to retain moisture, to keep the soil from getting too hot and to keep soil from splashing up on the lower leaves during rains and watering. Mulching also helps keep insects and disease from moving from the soil up into the plant. Use organic material such as wood chips, fine grass cuttings, straw (if you have a large garden), etc.

Growing Herbs Indoors

You can grow herbs indoors when it is too cold to grow them outside. Yields are usually smaller than from herbs grown outdoors, but you can still get decent results if you provide adequate light and moisture. Perennials, such as chives, oregano, mint and tarragon, seem to weather well and return in the spring with no problem. Other perennials, such as

> **Note**
>
> Do not leave lights on continuously, as herbs need darkness to perform photosynthesis. A duration of 14 to 16 hours a day is plenty to keep plants bushy.

> **Note**
>
> If manure is not available, fertilize every two weeks with liquid fish fertilizer or liquid seaweed. If manure is used, then fertilize once a month.

> **Note**
>
> Wash leaves a couple of hours after spraying to remove soap and any bugs that are not quite dead.

rosemary, thyme and parsley, may not. Herbs that are near a building or in a sheltered area have a better chance of survival where winters are harsh. Herbs such as lemon verbena must be dug up and stored indoors where temperatures go below freezing (they will lose their leaves), but may be returned to the garden the following season.

Herbs that do well indoors include basil, bay leaves, chives, dill, marjoram, mint, oregano, parsley, rosemary and sage.

Light
Choose a south- or west-facing window where plants will get at least five hours of direct sunlight per day. It can be difficult for plants to get sufficient light when days are short or overcast. If herbs start to look lanky, supplement light with two or more fluorescent grow lights above, perhaps attached under upper cupboards, or use an incandescent reflector grow lamp. Look for grow lights in your local nursery or plant store.

Temperature
Keep the temperature at 22°C to 25°C (72°F to 78°F) during the day; 18°C to 20°C (65°F to 68°F) during the night. Guard against cold drafts from windows. Pull curtains between windows and plants.

Moisture
Mist plants regularly; keep a minimum of 30 percent relative humidity (measure with hydrometer near plants). In winter use a room humidifier; kitchen steam from cooking and dishes is sometimes enough.

Watering
Herbs indoors need more frequent water than outdoor herbs. Don't let pots dry out completely—water when top 1 inch (2.5 cm) of soil is dry to the touch. Herbs in clay pots need to be watered more often. Make sure the soil is wet to the bottom of the pot but not water-logged; don't let herbs sit in water.

Soil
Combine equal parts sterilized potting soil, peat moss and perlite or sand with 1 tbsp (15 mL) composted, sterilized manure per 5-inch (12.5 cm) pot.

Or combine equal parts garden loam, builder's or silica sand and peat moss or leaf mold with 1 tbsp (15 mL) sterilized manure per 5-inch (12.5 cm) pot.

Insects
Misting regularly and rinsing weekly under the tap helps control bugs. Also good are Safer's Insecticidal Soap and Trounce (contains soap and pyrethrum—made from a plant of the daisy family); both are safe. Spray plants right after bringing indoors and keep away from other plants for the first few weeks.

Tips for Re-potting Herbs to Bring Indoors

- Minimize disturbance of the roots.
- Unglazed clay pots are best because they allow air to get to the roots.
- Re-pot herbs in late summer and let them remain outside for a few weeks to get used to the new pot.
- Bring herbs in for increasing lengths of time each day so they can get accustomed to lower levels of light.
- Cut leaves back so the amount of leaves is the same as the amount of roots (this will depend on the size of the pot).
- Water well, allowing good drainage; discard excess drained water.

How and When to Harvest Herbs

It is the aromatic (volatile) oils that give herbs their flavor, so we try to maximize and preserve the oils in harvesting. The best time to cut herbs is around mid-morning on a warm, dry day. The leaves must be clear of dew but the sun must be not so far advanced that the sun's heat has liberated the aromatic oils.

When cutting early in the season, do not take more than one-third of the plant. By mid-summer you can take about two-thirds without adversely affecting the growth. Use kitchen scissors and cut one-third of the way down the stem. This way of removing leaves encourages new growth.

Look at the plants carefully to see where the new growth is coming from. Leave small leaves to mature, taking larger leaves from further up the stem (towards the tip) and all around the plant. Harvest chives and parsley from the outside as their new growth comes from the center.

Avoid taking too much from perennials (see "Herb Directory," page 5) in their first season; allow them to get used to their surroundings and establish good roots.

Flavor is most potent if leaves are harvested just before flowering starts. Pluck flower buds/heads to prevent plants from going to seed.

How to Store and Handle Herbs

Herb leaves retain more flavor if left on stems until needed. (Do rinse off any dirt.) Store loosely in a plastic bag with stems wrapped in a damp paper towel; leave a little air in the bag. This will provide a moist environment for the herbs and prevent them from being crushed. Refrigerate.

Hearty herbs—ones with woody stems, such as rosemary and thyme—will store longer than soft leaf herbs—basil, cilantro, dill, etc. Some will keep up to two weeks. But try to use them as quickly as possible for maximum flavor.

When ready to use, rinse herbs well under running water or by swishing them in a bowl of water (or the bowl of a salad spinner). Some herbs such as cilantro and dill (particularly store-bought ones) can have quite a bit of sand on them. Take great care to ensure that all grit is removed or it will ruin any dish you add the herbs to. I rinse several times, until all traces of sand are gone (feel the bottom of the bowl; rinse the bowl in between).

I find the best way to dry herbs is with a salad spinner. It not only saves a lot of paper towel, it prevents over-handling and crushing of delicate leaves. The leaves will have a little water clinging to them; that is okay.

Once the herbs are fairly dry, place them in a length of good quality paper towel about three sections long. Fold the paper towel over to completely enclose the herbs; do this fairly loosely but snugly enough so they do not fall out. (There should be just a bit of dampness to the paper towel.) Place wrapped herbs inside a plastic bag and seal, leaving a bit of air inside the bag. Most herbs will keep like this, refrigerated, for a considerable time. Re-wrap herbs after opening. Check occasionally and remove any yellowed or wilted leaves and mist (or spray) the paper towel lightly to moisten if it becomes dry.

Freezing and Drying Herbs for Later Use

You can preserve the exquisite flavors from your summer herb garden, or deal with that excessive bunch of herbs from the grocery store quite easily. Some herbs lend themselves better to freezing, others are better dried; some are good both ways. The method you choose may depend on the intended use. My approach is that if herbs dry well (meaning that they retain a good flavor when dried), I dry them; if they don't, I freeze them. Flavor may be lost or changed with either method.

Freezing Herbs

Herbs that freeze well: basil, chives, cilantro, dill, mint, oregano, parsley, rosemary, sage, savory, tarragon, thyme.

When thawed they will be wilted but will retain most of their fresh flavor. Use good quality plastic freezer bags and plastic freezer storage containers to prevent flavor loss, freezer burn and transfer of odors from other foods. Frozen herbs will keep for four to six months.

Parsley

Remove clusters of parsley from their stems. Place in plastic freezer bag or plastic freezer container; freeze. To use, simply remove, chop and add to your dishes. (The result will not be good for garnishes.)

For large quantities, chop very dry parsley leaves in food processor and store in plastic freezer containers.

Chives

Snip chives at their base using scissors. Lay chives flat, in a single row on a large piece of plastic wrap. Roll up, leaving 2 inches (5 cm) to seal at end. Place in freezer bag for extra protection; freeze. (Cut chives to fit in freezer bags without bending.) To use, simply unroll and remove desired number of chives. These whole chives are perfect for tying appetizer bundles or wrapping around bunches of green beans or carrot sticks. Their limpness when thawed makes them like string.

Or snip chives using kitchen scissors into 1/2-inch (1 cm) lengths; place in plastic freezer container.

Basil

Remove leaves from stems, discarding any that are damaged. Pack leaves into plastic freezer bag or plastic freezer storage container; freeze. Also see "Herb Pastes" below.

Dill, Cilantro, Oregano, Rosemary, Tarragon

Remove smaller clusters of leaves from their stalks. Finely chop, then place 2 to 3 tsp (10 to 15 mL) in each section of an ice cube tray. Pour water over herbs to cover. Freeze, then transfer cubes to a freezer bag; label bag. To use, blocks may be dropped straight into soups and casseroles. To thaw, place on a piece of paper towel in the microwave oven for a few seconds, or leave at room temperature to thaw, then add to sauces or use as you would the fresh herb.

Herb Pastes

Another method for freezing is to purée the prepared leaves in a food processor with enough oil or olive oil to make a smooth paste. Use 2 cups (500 mL) herbs to 1/2 cup

(125 mL) oil plus 1/2 tsp (2 mL) salt. Transfer to small containers, cover with thin layer of oil. Freeze.

See also Basil Pesto (page 141).

Drying Herbs

Herbs that dry well include basil, dill, lemon verbena, marjoram, mint, oregano, rosemary, sage, savory, tarragon, thyme.

Drying concentrates the flavor of most herbs. As a herb is dried it loses volume, which is why you use only about one-third the amount of a dried herb in a recipe calling for fresh. The flavor of some herbs such as oregano actually improves with drying. Sage is also commonly used dried, although I have included recipes where it is used fresh. Some herbs lose their distinctive flavor when dried. I avoid using dried chives, cilantro and parsley, as their flavor is poor quality and does not resemble the fresh herb.

Paper Bag Drying

Gather the opening of a paper bag (approximately 10 × 6 inches/25 × 15 cm) around several stems held in one hand; fasten tightly around stems with elastic band or string. Poke a few holes in the bag for ventilation. Write the name of the herb and the date on the bag. Place the bag in a dry area or cupboard. (Do not store in the kitchen, which will have steam from cooking.) The amount of time herbs take to dry depends on the air dryness and quantity of herbs. (Do not overstuff bags, as air needs to circulate.)

In a week or two, the leaves should be completely dry. Test by crumbling some leaves; they should be crispy. Remove leaves from stems, leaving them whole. (Keep stems to throw on briquettes when barbecuing.)

See page 18 for How to Store.

Note

Watch carefully, as the paper towel can catch on fire. This has never happened to me—it seems to be related to the quality of paper towel used and excessive time in powerful microwave ovens. Just take it slowly and you will have no problems.

Microwave Drying

This is a very quick method that produces excellent results. Leaves may be slightly damp from washing. Arrange leaves in a single layer between a double thickness of good quality, plain paper towels. If drying a lot of herbs, use three pieces of paper towel on the bottom.

Microwave on high for one to two minutes. Remove from microwave, uncover and check to determine crispness. Move some herbs from center to the edges and edges to the center. The process will vary with the wattage of your microwave and if you have a turntable. If you do not have a turntable, turn paper towel 90 degrees when placing back into microwave.

Holding at the sides, flip the paper towel over. The damp paper towel from the bottom will now be on the top. Microwave on high for another minute or until leaves are dry and very crisp. Remove all crisp leaves; microwave any semi-crisp leaves until crisp. Try 15- to 30-second intervals. Do not microwave any longer than necessary, as flavor and color will be lost. Let rest until cooled.

Remove leaves from stems. (Keep stems to throw on briquettes when barbecuing.)

See below for How to Store.

How to Store Dried Herbs

1. Place completely dry herbs in a glass jar. Use airtight containers. Cover and label with the name of the herb and the date. Use jars sized so there is not a lot of excess air space.

2. Store in a cool, dry place, away from heat and light, such as inside a cupboard on a rack or small turntable.

3. Stored properly, dried herbs will take you through to the next season. To determine whether your herbs are still fresh enough, crumble a bit between your fingers. When you smell them, they should have a strong, recognizable fragrance. If they do not have their distinctive herb smell, they will not be very tasty; best to discard them. This freshness test goes for dried herbs that you purchase as well.

Note

Look for beautiful jars and labels in specialty kitchen stores. Recycle jars from other foods.

Useful Tips for Using Fresh Herbs

- Here's a quick way to chop fresh parsley. Place bunches in a 1-cup (250 mL) glass measure and chop with kitchen scissors, especially the spring-loaded kind. When done, jiggle the container to level the chopped herb and check measurement. Easy clean-up too!

- Use a food processor to chop large quantities of parsley.
- Create a chiffonade (translates literally as "made of rags") of herbs for sprinkling over salads, soups, etc. Take large whole leaves of herbs such as basil, mint or sage, place one on top of the other, roll up along their length, hold tight and slice into thin shreds.
- Use kitchen scissors to snip fresh chives into 1/2-inch (1 cm) lengths; store about 1/2 cup (125 mL) of them in a small covered bowl or plastic container. They will keep in the refrigerator several days. Use to sprinkle on vegetables, salads and omelettes.

Herb Vinegars

Making herb vinegars is an extremely easy way to capture the flavor of herbs. These fragrant vinegars are sprinkled over hot vegetables, spritzed on fish in place of lemon juice, added to soups and stews; they are used in marinades, to make salad dressings, mayonnaise and sauces; in place of lemon or lime juice in drinks and salsas; in pickles and chutneys.

Recycle and re-use glass bottles from liquor and commercial sauces. Ask friends or local bars to save bottles for you (some brands of scotch and imported beers come in beautiful bottles). Some kitchen stores carry decorative glass bottles with corks. I have also purchased small wine bottles from make-your-own wine stores. I prefer bottles with broad bases instead of tall, narrow ones, which can tip over. Clear glass is best for pretty colored vinegars, such as chive flower or purple basil, and to show off herb sprigs in vinegars made with lighter-colored vinegars. Ones made with red wine vinegar or many combined herbs can come out an unattractive brownish color and are better in dark brown or green bottles.

For gift-giving, you can find rubber stamps with herbs to make pretty labels. The tops of the corks can be sealed with wax or with the plastic seals used to top wine bottles (from make-your-own wine stores). These small plastic covers go loosely onto the bottle top then are heated with a heat gun or boiling kettle to shrink on tightly. Use raffia to tie a small label to the neck with usage ideas or a recipe. Place the bottle in a fancy liquor store gift bag with tissue or put in a basket with a bottle of herb oil.

Making Herb Vinegars

Vinegar

A good quality white wine vinegar will do for any herb. Delicate herbs (dill, chervil, cilantro) are better with lighter vinegars, such as rice wine or white wine vinegar. The more pungent herbs (sage, savory, rosemary, thyme) suit stronger-flavored vinegars (red wine, apple cider). Vinegar should be a minimum 5 percent acetic acid by volume (this information is usually written on the label).

Clear distilled (white) vinegar is ideal for making vinegars from flowers of chives, nasturtiums, violets, roses and carnations, as well as purple basil, where a clean color is desired. Remove the bitter green base from the flowers. (See page 38 on Edible Flowers.)

Note

Don't worry about using too much herb. If the final result is strongly flavored, you can always add more vinegar to it, or add plain vinegar when you are making something with it.

Herbs

Do not use dried herbs to make herb vinegars.

I like to make single herb vinegars, then blend them when cooking for a unique taste. For instance, if a dressing recipe calls for 3 tbsp (45 mL) vinegar, I may use 1 tbsp (15 mL) of purple basil vinegar and 2 tbsp (30 mL) of chive flower vinegar. One of my other standard vinegars is tarragon.

I steep the vinegar first, then strain and discard the spent herbs. I add fresh herbs for decorative purposes when giving the vinegar as a gift, or to identify a single herb vinegar, e.g., a sprig of tarragon in tarragon vinegar. Bottle close to the time you are giving so the herb or herb flower sprig(s) you add will retain their bright color(s). Once the herb is in the vinegar, the color will start to leach out.

Additions

You may add garlic, peppercorns, chili peppers, citrus peel or herb seeds to your vinegars. Use the hot method (see below) if adding any of these.

To add whole garlic cloves, arrange them on a wooden skewer, checking to make sure they will fit through the opening of your bottle. Peel citrus zest in one piece, using a vegetable peeler or knife; thread onto a wooden skewer. Insert skewer into jar before adding vinegar.

Storing

Label and date bottled vinegars. Store in a cool, dark place. Unopened, most vinegars will last a year or two. Once opened, use up within six months. If you are not sure if a vinegar is still usable, trust your taste. If it does not have a distinctive herb taste, chances are most of the flavor has been lost. Discard any vinegars that have fungus growth on the surface.

Hot Method (48 hours)

Rinse and pat dry herbs. Half fill a clean large glass jar (preferably a large canning jar) with chopped or torn herbs. Remove leaves from herbs with thick or woody stems, such as basil, rosemary or sage; leave very small herb leaves such as thyme on stems (too fussy to remove). Heat vinegar in the microwave or in a non-reactive saucepan. Whole spices, such as peppercorns, can be heated with the vinegar. Do not boil. Pour hot vinegar over herbs. Cool to room temperature; cover with plastic lids (vinegar will corrode metal lids) and steep for 48 hours in a cool, dark place. Do not sit jars in a sunny window, as heat and light will destroy flavor.

The vinegar is now ready to use, but the flavor will continue to develop for another couple of weeks. Test for flavor and, if it is to your liking, strain (discard herbs) and pour into smaller bottles with a fresh sprig of herb in each. Seal with non-metallic lids; label and date bottles.

Cold Method (2 to 3 weeks)

This method takes longer but produces a clear, mellow flavor. Prepare the herbs as you would for the hot method, but do not heat the vinegar. Check after two days. If herbs are not completely submerged, add more vinegar. Leave another three to four weeks, then strain into smaller jars or bottles. Insert a fresh sprig of herb in each jar or bottle. Seal with non-metallic lids; label and date.

Recipes for Herb Vinegar

Add the following to 3 cups (750 mL) vinegar.

Basil Garlic Vinegar

For salads, egg dishes, tomatoes, beef, chicken, cauliflower, broccoli:

6 to 8	fresh basil sprigs 6 to 8
4	large garlic cloves 4 (or 1/4 cup/60mL chopped garlic chives)
	black peppercorns, optional
	white wine vinegar

Oregano Garlic Vinegar

For meat marinades, grilled vegetables, Italian dishes:

6 to 8	fresh oregano sprigs 6 to 8
4	large garlic cloves 4 (or 1/4 cup/60 mL chopped garlic chives)
	black peppercorns, optional
	white wine vinegar

Rosemary Garlic Vinegar

For chicken, pork, lamb, potato salad:

3 or 4	fresh rosemary sprigs 3 or 4
4	large garlic cloves 4 (or 1/4 cup/60mL chopped garlic chives)
	cider vinegar

Rosemary Orange Vinegar

For chicken, pork, lamb:

3 or 4	fresh rosemary sprigs 3 or 4
	zest of 1 orange
	white wine vinegar

Lemon Tarragon Vinegar

For fish, seafood, chicken:

4 to 6	fresh tarragon sprigs 4 to 6
	rind of 1 lemon
	white wine vinegar

Dill Lemon Vinegar

For fish/seafood, vegetables, potato salad:

4 to 6	fresh dill sprigs 4 to 6
	rind of 1 lemon
1 tsp	mustard seed 5 mL
	rice wine vinegar

Red Wine Herb Vinegar

For marinades, salads:

2 or 3	sprigs each of three of the following: fresh basil, oregano, rosemary, thyme or lemon thyme, marjoram, savory 2 or 3
	red wine vinegar

Mixed Herb Vinegar

For chicken salad, fish, vegetables:

1 to 1-1/2 cups	finely chopped fresh herbs: basil, parsley, dill, thyme, tarragon, rosemary, summer savory, marjoram 250 to 375 mL
2 to 3	garlic cloves 2 to 3 (or 1/4 cup/60 mL chopped garlic chives)
1 tsp	black peppercorns 5 mL
	white wine or cider vinegar

Italian Herb Vinegar

For marinades, soups, stews, salads:

1/2 cup	each: chopped fresh rosemary and thyme	125 mL
1/4 cup	each: chopped fresh chives and oregano	60 mL
1	sprig fresh Italian parsley, chopped	1
1/2 cup	chopped shallots	125 mL
12	black peppercorns	12
	white wine vinegar	

Fines Herbes Vinegar

For fish, seafood, vegetables:

1/2 cup	each: chopped fresh chervil, chives, parsley and tarragon	125 mL
	white wine vinegar	

Lavender Vinegar

For marinating red meat, salad dressing:

4 tsp	fresh lavender flowers	20 mL
	(or 2 tsp/5 mL dried)	
	white wine vinegar	

Other combinations

- cilantro, fresh ginger, chili pepper, rice wine vinegar
- oregano, sage, rosemary, lemon thyme, peppercorns, red wine vinegar
- oregano, mustard seeds, peppercorns, whole cloves, white wine vinegar
- tarragon, green peppercorns, white wine vinegar
- tarragon, dill and garlic, white wine vinegar
- rosemary, mint, red wine vinegar
- rosemary, lemon thyme, white wine vinegar

Recipes Using Herb Vinegars

Salad Dressings

1/3 cup	Herb Vinegar 75 mL
1 cup	oil 250 mL
1 tsp	each: granulated sugar, Dijon mustard 5 mL

Whisk together or blend in food processor or blender.

Creamy Herb Dressing

1/3 cup	Herb Vinegar 75 mL
2/3 cup	oil 150 mL
1/3 cup	sour cream 75 mL
1 tbsp	granulated sugar 15 mL
1/2 tsp	each: dry mustard and paprika 2 mL

Whisk together or blend in food processor or blender.

Marinades

1/3 cup	each: Herb Vinegar, oil, wine 75 mL

Whisk together and pour over meat in a glass dish or plastic bag. Cover and marinate in refrigerator.

Herbed Mayonnaise

1	egg 1
3/4 cup	oil 175 mL
2 tbsp	Herb Vinegar 30 mL
1/4 tsp	dry mustard 1 mL (or 1 tsp/5 mL Dijon mustard)
1	clove garlic, minced, optional 1
1/4 tsp	salt 1 mL

Note

Works best if oil is at room temperature.

In food processor or blender, combine egg, 1/4 cup (60 mL) of the oil, Herb Vinegar, mustard, garlic (if using) and salt. Pulse 15 to 30 seconds to mix well. Very slowly drizzle in the remaining 1/2 cup (125 mL) of the oil in a thin stream until it thickens; scrape down sides once all of the oil has been added. Place in glass jar and store in refrigerator for up to 4 days.

Herb Oils

The flavorful, volatile oils from herbs infuse nicely into cooking oils. Use herbs such as basil, cilantro, dill, marjoram, mint, oregano, rosemary, sage, savory, tarragon and thyme, by themselves or in combination. I prefer to make single herb oils, and then combine them when I am cooking. This allows for the most flexibility.

Herb oils have a concentrated flavor so only small amounts are needed. A little bit of herb oil will give a rich taste to low-fat meals. They add flavor to healthy foods like fish, vegetables and grains, which are typically low in fat to begin with.

Oils do not contain any cholesterol (cholesterol comes mainly from animal-source fats). Some oils have actually been found to assist in reducing the LDL-cholesterol in the blood and to maintain healthy levels of HDL-cholesterol. Fresh oils are a good source of unsaturated fat and essential fats, which must be obtained from food.

Suggestions for Using Herb Oils

- in marinades, mayonnaise, sauces
- in grain, bean or pasta salads, salad dressings
- drizzled over cooked or grilled vegetables
- to cook mushrooms or stir-fry vegetables
- with a little balsamic vinegar for dipping bread
- on pizza dough or drizzled over cooked pizza; to flavor pasta
- to flavor croutons for salads and soups
- brushed on toasted crostini for appetizers or to make breadcrumbs for gratins
- to marinate cheeses, such as goat cheese
- drizzled over tomato halves before broiling
- brushed over the top of bread, rolls, etc., before warming

Making Herb Oils

I like to use neutral-flavored oils such as safflower, sunflower, canola and light olive oil, for making herb oils. These oils allow the taste of the herb to shine through. However, regular olive oil or peanut oil may be suitable, depending on the end use of your oil. For Greek salad, you may wish to infuse olive oil with fresh oregano or, for a stir-fry, peanut oil with cilantro.

By using a good ratio of herbs to oil—about 1:2—the oil will develop an intense flavor, and not as much oil will need to be used in your recipes and cooking.

Store oils in the refrigerator, covered, in a glass jar or bottle; use within a month. Oils may become cloudy when cold but will clear once they come to room temperature.

Make small batches and use up as quickly as possible.

Method 1: Infusing

1. Rinse herbs well with cold water and blot dry (they should be completely dry).
2. Tear or coarsely chop leaves and pack loosely into a sterilized, large wide-mouth jar, such as a large canning jar. (Remove large leaves like basil from their stems first.) Fill jar about half-full of herbs.
3. Pour oil over herbs to cover; seal and store in refrigerator for 1 week.
4. Pour off oil into a clean jar (or strain) and discard herbs. Taste oil. If a stronger flavor is desired, repeat, using new herbs. Once desired flavor is reached pour into decorative or other glass bottle with a cap. Store in refrigerator up to six months. (Refrigeration prevents rancidity. Rancid oil has a strong paint-like smell.)

Method 2: Puréeing

1. Prepare herbs as in Method 1.
2. In a food processor, finely chop 1-1/2 cups (375 mL) loosely packed herbs; slowly pour in 2 cups (500 mL) oil with processor running.
3. Store in fridge; use within 1 week. To keep longer, strain out herbs, tightly cover and store in refrigerator for up to a month.

Method 3: Heating

This method is used when you are adding spices, fresh ginger or sun-dried tomatoes to the oil.

1. Prepare herbs as in Method 1.

Caution

Oil infusions that contain garlic must be kept refrigerated, as they are susceptible to botulism (*clostridium botulinum*). To be safe, add garlic to a portion of oil only a few hours before using; keep refrigerated. Discard unused oil after 1 week.

Note

Always start with a fresh, unopened bottle of oil.

Note

Method 2 produces an oil that is greenish in color with a slightly sharper flavor (like the effect of squeezing a teabag when making a cup of tea). However, it is a quick way to extract the flavor, and the oil can be used right away if desired.

2. Heat oil and spices in a small, heavy-bottom saucepan or in a large glass measuring cup in microwave, just until hot. DO NOT BOIL.

3. Stir in herbs; let stand at room temperature until cool. Strain through a fine sieve; discard solids. Pour oil into a clean glass jar or bottle; cover and refrigerate for up to a month.

Additions

- dried chili peppers
- peppercorns
- whole spices such as cloves, cardamom, cinnamon stick, star anise
- ground spices such as ginger, saffron, cumin
- herb seeds such as dill seed, fennel, coriander and caraway

Oil Blends

Here are just a few suggestions to try. Customize your oils to suit your own tastes and uses.

Dill and Lemon: fresh dill, dill seed, lemon rind

Fines Herbes: fresh chervil, chives, parsley and tarragon

Rosemary and Orange: fresh rosemary, orange rind, hot red pepper flakes

Savory: fresh rosemary, thyme and sage, shallots, black peppercorns

Sun-Dried Tomato and Oregano: fresh oregano or marjoram, sun-dried tomatoes, garlic (also good made with fresh basil)

Herb Mustards

Mustard is such a versatile and staple cooking ingredient that it is ideal for capturing the flavor of fresh herbs. Mustards can be used as sandwich spreads, added to hot and cold sauces, butters, marinades, salad dressings and devilled eggs, or simply used as a condiment to meats, such sausages.

The easiest way to make herb mustards is to begin with a good quality mustard such as Dijon mustard, grainy mustard or deli-style mustard. Choose the mustard that has the sharpness or sweetness that you like. You can make your own from scratch using mustard seeds, but that is a lot of work, and will not be covered in this book.

To make mustards using dry mustard, combine equal amounts of dry mustard with white wine or herb vinegar to make a paste. Stir in minced garlic or shallots and some minced mixed herbs. If desired, add a little honey or brown sugar to taste.

Try small batches to start, using about 1 cup (250 mL) mustard. You can taste it to see if you like it, or make several to have on hand. I prefer to make single herb mustards, such as tarragon or dill, to use as ingredients in salad dressings, mayonnaise or sandwich spreads.

Soft-leaf herbs, such as basil, chervil, cilantro, dill, savory, sage and tarragon, can be minced and stirred into the mustard. The flavor will take several days to develop. Store in the refrigerator up to six months. Use only coated or plastic lids, as the vinegar in the mustard will corrode metal lids. Be sure to label with the herb used and the date.

Basic Recipe for Mixed Herb Mustard

1 cup	Dijon mustard	250 mL
2 tbsp	minced fresh parsley	30 mL
1 tbsp	minced fresh tarragon	15 mL
2 tsp	minced fresh basil	10 mL
2 tsp	minced fresh dill	10 mL
2 tsp	minced fresh oregano	10 mL

1. In a small bowl, mix together all ingredients.
2. Place mixture in a jar; cover and refrigerate for 2 to 3 days before using.

Makes about 1-1/4 cups (300 mL).

Recipes for Herb Mustards

Fines Herbes Mustard

1 cup	Dijon mustard	250 mL
1 tbsp	each: minced chives and parsley	15 mL
2 tsp	each: minced chervil and tarragon	10 mL

Method as above.

Makes about 1 cup (250 mL).

Italian Mustard

1 cup	Dijon mustard	250 mL
2 tbsp	minced fresh basil	30 mL
1 tbsp	minced fresh oregano	15 mL
1 tsp	balsamic vinegar	5 mL

Method as above.

Makes about 1 cup (250 mL).

Pesto Mustard

| 1 cup | Dijon mustard 250 mL |
| 1/4 cup | Basil Pesto (see page 141) 60 mL |

Method as above.

Makes about 1-1/4 cups (300 mL).

Lavender Mustard

1/2 cup	Dijon mustard 125 mL
2 tsp	fresh lavender flowers 10 mL
	(or 1 tsp/5 mL dried)
1 tsp	honey 5 mL

Method as above.

Makes about 1/2 cup (125 mL).

<table>
<tr><td>

Variation
Use red wine in place of white and 1/4 cup (60 mL) chopped fresh basil in place of rosemary and tarragon.

</td><td>

Rosemary Tarragon Mustard

This method works better for tougher herbs such as rosemary.

1/4 cup	dry white wine 60 mL
2 tbsp	minced shallots 30 mL
1 tbsp	finely chopped fresh rosemary 15 mL
1 tbsp	finely chopped fresh tarragon 15 mL
1 cup	Dijon mustard 250 mL

</td></tr>
</table>

1. In a small saucepan, combine wine, shallots and herbs over high heat. Bring to a boil; reduce heat and simmer until the liquid has been reduced by half. Strain through a fine sieve; discard solids.

2. In a small bowl, mix mustard with herbed wine. Place in a jar; cover and refrigerate for 2 to 3 days before using.

Makes about 1 cup (250 mL).

Herb Butters

Butter is another good medium for capturing the flavor of fresh herbs. Butters can be made for immediate use, but I like to freeze them too. Herbs frozen in butter keep their freshness better than if frozen on their own. Use salted or unsalted butter. If you wish, you can make herb butters using a good quality margarine (I prefer the non-hydrogenated types).

I am not suggesting that we slather our food with butter, but we can allow ourselves a little to add interesting herb flavors to low-fat foods such as vegetables, fish, chicken, lean pork and grilled meats.

Spread herb butters on fresh bread or rolls. They are excellent spread on French bread slices and heated in the oven for a few minutes. Or toss toasted bread cubes in melted herb butter for savory croutons. Use them to enhance the taste of vegetables by tossing a little onto hot vegetables and shaking to coat; see the chart of herbs and vegetables on page 161. Use chive, marjoram or rosemary butter on corn-on-the-cob or to top baked potatoes.

Butters may also be used to make pastry crusts for sweet or savory dishes, such as tarts or quiches.

Making Herb Butters

Herb butters are quite easy to prepare. For large batches using 1 lb/500 g butter, use a food processor. First, chop the rinsed and well-dried herb leaves in the food processor, then add the butter and any additional ingredients, such as mustard, garlic, shallots, lemon juice, etc. Add a little olive or sunflower oil to the butter, if desired.

If you are using edible flowers for your butter (see "Edible Flowers," page 38), stir in by hand for a prettier look. Flowers from herbs such as chives, garlic chives and basil are nice additions to butters.

For small quantities, finely chop herb leaves (removed from stems) and blend well into softened butter. I just stir them together in a medium bowl.

Butters may be packed into small plastic freezer storage containers. You can wrap them with plastic wrap in logs, and then over-wrap in plastic freezer bags or place in a rectangular storage container. Wrap them well so they do not pick up (or transfer) odors in your freezer.

Storage
Refrigerate for one to two weeks (unsalted butter is more perishable); freeze for up to six months.

Butter
For convenience, I like to use butter sold in sticks. Each stick is equivalent to 1/2 cup (125 mL), 4 oz (125 g) or one-quarter of a pound. Unwrap butter from foil paper while it is still cold and it will come off the paper easily. Place in bowl to soften.

Basic Recipe for Herb Butter

Prepare at least two hours ahead to allow flavors to blend.

1/2 cup	softened butter	125 mL
2 tbsp	finely chopped fresh herbs	30 mL
1 tbsp	finely chopped fresh parsley, optional	15 mL

1. In a medium bowl or food processor, mix together butter and herbs until well combined.

2. Spoon mixture onto a piece of plastic wrap or waxed paper. Shape into a log or cylinder about 1-1/2 inches (3.5 cm) in diameter, and twist ends to secure. If using waxed paper, store in a plastic bag or wrap; label.

3. Refrigerate until firm or freeze for later use.

To use, allow to soften a bit then slice 1/4 inch (5 mm) thick and place on top of food. The heat of the food will slowly melt the butter.

Recipes and Uses for Herb Butters

Add the following ingredients to the Basic Recipe:

Parsley Butter (Maître d'Hôtel Butter)

Use on any vegetables or grilled steak. For fish, use 2 tsp (10 mL) finely chopped shallots in place of garlic, or use finely chopped coriander in place of parsley and omit garlic.

2 tbsp	finely chopped fresh parsley (Italian or curly)	30 mL
1	clove garlic, crushed	1
2 tsp	lemon juice	10 mL
pinch	black pepper	pinch

Fines Herbes Butter

Use with fish, chicken or eggs; with vegetables such as peas, green beans, asparagus, potatoes.

1 tbsp	each: finely chopped fresh chervil, chives, parsley and tarragon	15 mL
1 tbsp	finely chopped shallots, optional	15 mL

Lemon Dill Butter

Use with fish/seafood or vegetables such as asparagus, beets, potatoes, tomatoes, spinach.

2 tbsp	finely chopped fresh dill	30 mL
2 tsp	lemon or lime juice	10 mL

Tarragon-Dijon Butter

Use on grilled steak (gives the taste of Bernaise sauce) or fish; with vegetables such as green beans, carrots, asparagus, peas, tomatoes, mushrooms.

1 tbsp	finely chopped fresh tarragon	15 mL
1 tbsp	finely chopped fresh parsley	15 mL
1	clove garlic, crushed	1
1 tsp	lemon juice	5 mL
1 tsp	Dijon mustard	5 mL

Basil-Oregano-Thyme Garlic Butter

Excellent for garlic bread and croutons; use with eggs or vegetables such as roasted sweet peppers, eggplant, broccoli, zucchini, potatoes, tomatoes.

2 tbsp	finely chopped fresh basil	30 mL
2 tsp	finely chopped fresh oregano	10 mL
1/2 tsp	finely chopped fresh thyme	2 mL
1	clove garlic, crushed	1

Rosemary Butter

Use with lamb, beef or chicken; with squash. For vegetables such as potatoes, cauliflower, mushrooms and squash, omit orange rind and pepper; add 1 tbsp (15 mL) each parsley and chives or garlic chives.

1 tbsp	finely chopped fresh rosemary	15 mL
2 tsp	grated orange rind	10 mL
1/2 tsp	coarsely ground black pepper	2 mL

Tomato Marjoram Butter

Use with fresh vegetables, especially zucchini; with fish and lamb. For pasta, rice, chicken and fish, use 1 tbsp (15 mL) each basil and oregano in place of marjoram.

2 tbsp	finely chopped fresh marjoram	30 mL
	(or 1 tbsp/15 mL chopped fresh oregano)	
1 tbsp	tomato paste	15 mL
1 tsp	lemon juice	5 mL
	Black pepper, optional	

Basil Sun-Dried Tomato Butter

Spread on bread and broil until bubbly; serve with pasta or vegetables such as green beans, zucchini.

2 tbsp	finely chopped fresh basil	30 mL
1 tbsp	minced, softened sun-dried tomatoes (softened)	15 mL
1 tbsp	freshly grated Parmesan cheese	15 mL
2 tsp	minced shallots	10 mL
1	small clove garlic, crushed	1

Roasted Pepper Oregano Butter

Use on pasta or vegetables such as cauliflower, cabbage, green beans, Brussels sprouts, zucchini.

2 tbsp	minced roasted sweet red or yellow peppers	30 mL
1 tbsp	finely chopped fresh oregano or marjoram	15 mL
1	small clove garlic, crushed	1
pinch	hot red pepper flakes, optional	pinch

Pesto Butter

Use for fish, shrimp or vegetables such as zucchini, grilled tomatoes, eggplant.

1/2 cup	Basil Pesto (see page 141)	125 mL

Sage Butter

Use with pork, chicken, turkey or veal; with vegetables such as cabbage, corn, sautéed onions, green beans, potatoes. For beef or vegetables such as asparagus, green beans, eggplant, peas, squash, use savory in place of sage.

2 tbsp	finely chopped fresh sage	30 mL
1 tbsp	finely chopped fresh parsley	15 mL
2 tsp	finely chopped shallots	10 mL

Chive Flower Butter

Use to butter cucumber sandwiches or biscuits.

2 tbsp	chive flower florets	30 mL
1 tbsp	finely chopped fresh parsley, optional	15 mL

Chive Ginger Butter

Use on squash or sweet potatoes. May also be made without fresh ginger and served with almost any vegetable.

2 tbsp	finely chopped fresh chives	30 mL
1 tbsp	finely chopped fresh parsley or cilantro	15 mL
1 tbsp	finely grated fresh ginger	15 mL
1 tsp	lemon or lime juice	5 mL
pinch	black pepper	pinch

Cilantro Chili Butter

Use with chicken, pork, shrimp, eggs, rice or vegetables such as green beans, carrots, corn, potatoes, zucchini.

2 tbsp	finely chopped fresh cilantro	30 mL
1 tbsp	finely chopped fresh parsley	15 mL
2 tsp	minced jalapeño or other chili pepper	10 mL
	(or 1/4 tsp/1 mL hot red pepper flakes)	
1/2 tsp	ground cumin	2 mL

Cilantro Lime Butter

Use with grilled fish/seafood, chicken or beef, or to butter corn-on-the-cob.

3 tbsp	finely chopped fresh cilantro	45 mL
1 tbsp	lime juice	15 mL
1/2 tsp	finely grated lime rind	2 mL
pinch	hot red pepper flakes, optional	pinch

Garden Harvest Butter

Use with beef, chicken, fish, eggs or vegetables such as carrots, tomatoes, potatoes.

1 tbsp	each: finely chopped fresh tarragon, parsley	15 mL
2 tsp	finely chopped fresh thyme or lemon thyme	10 mL
2 tsp	finely chopped fresh oregano	10 mL
pinch	black pepper	pinch

Basil and Nutmeg Butter

Use for vegetables such as cauliflower, squash, green beans, spinach. Use cinnamon basil or purple basil in place of regular basil; omit nutmeg.

2 tbsp	finely chopped fresh basil	30 mL
1/4 tsp	ground nutmeg	1 mL
pinch	black pepper	pinch

Variation

Orange Mint and Shallot Butter: Use 1 tbsp (15 mL) orange mint, omit parsley and garlic; add 2 tbsp (30 mL) minced shallots.

Mint Butter

Use with lamb, swordfish or vegetables such as peas, grilled tomatoes, green beans, carrots.

2 tbsp	finely chopped fresh mint 30 mL (see note on Mints, page 7)	
1 tbsp	finely chopped fresh parsley	15 mL
1	small clove garlic, crushed	1

Herb Flower Butter

Serve with poached or grilled fish such as salmon, trout or tuna.

1 tbsp	each: chive, basil, dill and rosemary flowers	15 mL
1 tbsp	finely chopped purple basil leaves	15 mL
1 tsp	lemon juice	5 mL

Edible Flower Butter

See page 38 for Edible Flowers. Use to butter scones, to make tart pastry or in shortbread cookies.

2 tbsp	chopped mixed edible flower petals	30 mL
2 tsp	liquid honey, optional	10 mL

Nasturtium Flower Butter

Use this peppery-tasting butter with fish and any vegetables you wish.

1/2 cup	chopped nasturtium flower petals (orange, yellow, red) and leaves	125 mL
1 tbsp	minced shallots	15 mL

Special Serving Presentations

- Roll small balls of butter (about 2 tsp/10 mL each) in finely chopped parsley or chives; chill.
- Use a melon baller to make rounds from semi-firm butters; drop into ice water. Remove from ice water, arrange on serving dish or freeze on a baking sheet then transfer to plastic freezer bags.
- Logs may be rolled in finely chopped parsley or chives, then sliced 1/4 inch (5 mm) thick and placed on waxed paper to chill. If using frozen logs, thaw slightly and parsley will stick more easily.
- For cut-out shapes, roll butter between two pieces of waxed paper to 1/4-inch (5 mm) thickness; chill until firm. Use small cookie or canape cutters to cut into decorative or festive shapes (hearts, maple leaves, flowers).
- Make butter in food processor, then use a pastry bag fitted with a large star tip to pipe onto a baking sheet lined with waxed paper; chill. Use a thin metal spatula to remove.
- Pack butter into small molds and chill. Tiny molds used for chocolate making are also good for this.
- Whip butter until light and fluffy, then spoon gently into small individual ramekins. Sprinkle with finely chopped parsley or chive flowers.
- Decorate serving plate with herb sprigs and edible flowers.

Herb Honeys

Herb honeys are great to use in cooking, as well as to stir into hot drinks such as tea or cold drinks like lemonade, punch or champagne. When serving cold drinks, a few fresh lemon verbena or mint leaves can be added to the glass or frozen in ice cubes. Use herb honey to sweeten fruit salads, stir it into fruit salad or yogurt, add a small amount to a salad dressing or use it to replace regular honey in baking.

Making Herb Honeys

Simply heat 1 cup (250 mL) honey in a small saucepan over low heat, stirring, or in a large glass measure in the microwave. Stir in about 1/4 cup (60 mL) finely chopped fresh herbs, such as lemon thyme, lemon verbena, lemon balm, cinnamon basil, orange mint, rosemary, sage, lavender flowers, rose- or lemon-scented geranium. Cover and let rest at room temperature for about one week.

Taste honey. It may need to be left a few days longer or to be re-infused with more fresh herbs. If necessary to re-infuse to strengthen the flavor, stir in about 2 tbsp (30 mL) chopped fresh herbs and repeat as above. When the desired flavor is reached, re-warm the honey in a saucepan or the microwave, stirring. Pour through a fine sieve; discard solids.

Herb Syrups

Herb syrups can be used in much the same way as herb honey, but they can also be used to glaze the top of loaves, muffins, etc. After baking, let loaf cool in pan for about ten minutes. Brush syrup over top of loaf; turn loaf out onto cooling rack and cool completely.

Lavender syrup is great in sparkling wine with slices of strawberries. Add one vanilla bean, split lengthwise, to lavender syrup and use it to pour over fruit, such as peaches, raspberries, strawberries or blueberries.

Other herbs to use for syrups are the same as those used to make Herb Honeys (see above).

Variations

- Use 1 cup (250 mL) dry white wine and 1/4 cup (60 mL) water in place of the 1 cup (250 mL) water. This syrup is tasty over fresh fruit as a dessert.
- Use orange juice in place of water and pour over citrus fruit salad, melons or cantaloupe.

Rosemary Syrup

1-1/2 cups	water	375 mL
1 cup	granulated sugar	250 mL
1/3 cup	packed fresh rosemary leaves	
	(or other herbs or herb flowers	
	listed above under Herb Honeys)	75 mL
	Whole spices such as cinnamon or	
	cloves, optional	
	Lemon or orange rind, optional	

1. In a small saucepan, combine water, sugar and rosemary. Bring to a boil over high heat. Reduce heat; cover and simmer for 5 minutes. Remove from heat; let stand 30 minutes.

2. Strain through a fine sieve; discard solids. Refrigerate in a glass bottle or jar for up to 2 months. (For half the recipe, use 3 tbsp/45 mL chopped fresh herbs.)

Makes 2 cups (500 mL).

Herb Sugars

Herbs will impart their flavors to sugar, too, which can then be used to make cookies, cakes, pies, etc.; sprinkled over fruit or cereal; used to top cookies, scones or muffins and to sweeten hot or cold drinks.

In a jar, layer whole herb leaves (cinnamon basil, mints, rosemary, lemon verbena, lemon balm, rose or lemon geranium, lavender, etc.) with about 1/4 cup (60 mL) granulated sugar (extra-fine if possible) between each layer. Cover and let rest at room temperature for about a week. Sift through strainer to remove herbs. (Sugar may have hardened slightly.) Keep in covered glass jar up to a year.

Herb Jams, Jellies and Chutneys

Herbs add great flavor to preserves. They can be used as condiments to meats, eaten on scones, brushed over fruit tarts, eaten with cream cheese on crackers. See my first book, *Prizewinning Preserves* (2001, Prentice Hall), for recipes for Strawberry Lavender and Peach Lavender Jams, Lavender Jelly, Purple Basil Wine Jelly, Mint and Pineapple Mint Jellies, Rosemary Apple Cider Jelly, Cran-Apple Sage Chutney.

Edible Flowers

Although the presence of flowers in a salad surprises many people, the use of wild and cultivated flowers in salads is one of the nicest traditions we have inherited from the past. The flowers do not impart a lot of flavor; however, the unexpected color adds interest to a salad.

There are lots of edible flowers available to the adventurous cook, but be sure to identify them accurately; if you are in doubt, leave them out of the salad altogether. Before using them in salad, wash flowers very lightly (swish in water to remove any garden pests); pat dry with paper towel.

It is preferable to use home-grown flowers, avoiding those that grow close to the road or are commercially sprayed with herbicides or pesticides. (Never use cut flowers from florists or fruit markets.) Many stores now carry edible flowers such as pansies or nasturtiums.

Vibrant, healthy flowers will have the best flavor. To store flowers overnight, spray them with water and place in plastic bags in the refrigerator.

Edible flowers include:

Apple	Honeysuckle
Borage	Jasmine
Carnation	Lavender
Chrysanthemum	Lemon Blossom
Daisy	Lilac
Dandelion	Marigold
Daylily	Nasturtium and its leaves
Elderberry flowers	Pansy
Geranium	Rose
Gladioli	Tulip
Hibiscus	Violet and its leaves
Hollyhock	Flowers of culinary herbs

Tips for Using Edible Flowers

- Marigolds make a good, inexpensive substitute for saffron, and impart a lovely golden color to rice.
- Borage flowers, roses and violets make refreshing drinks. Soak flowers in chilled water for several hours; strain out flowers and serve with fresh blossoms floating in each glass.
- Freeze small flowers in ice cubes for drinks or in a ring mold to float in a punch bowl: fill ice-cube trays or a ring mold half-full with water, add flowers and freeze; add more flowers and water and freeze again.
- Carnations, chrysanthemums, nasturtiums or herb flowers are ideal for blending with butter, to make flower butters. Herb flowers add delicious flavor to breads; try rosemary, sage or thyme.

- Use edible flowers to garnish soups (chive and other herb flowers) and desserts (violets, roses, carnations, lavender).
- Include flowers in green salads, either whole or as confetti (mixed flower petals).

Herb Seeds

Some of the fresh herbs of the *umbellifer* family—dill, parsley, cumin, coriander, caraway and fennel—produce flavorful seeds. The flowers, which resemble tiny umbrellas, turn into green berries, then dry to brown seeds within approximately ten days. These can then be picked and stored, preferably in a glass jar, and kept for up to a year. Their flavor is more intense than the leaves due to the oils they contain. Some seeds, like coriander seed, have an entirely different flavor from the fresh herb (also known as cilantro, Chinese parsley or fresh coriander).

Herb seeds can be used to flavor pickles, breads, meats, fish and flavored oils.

Seeds may be planted to grow more fresh herbs for the next season. Plants will drop some of their seeds, which will come up on their own the next summer. For a continuous supply of fresh cilantro, plant seeds at one-week intervals.

Caraway Seed
Warm, pungent, slightly bitter flavor with aniseed overtones. Complements cabbage, coleslaw, sauerkraut, potatoes, onions, carrots, pickles, cheese, goulash, pork, rye bread, cakes, biscuits and dumplings.

Coriander Seed
Mild, sweet, slightly pungent, citrus-like flavor with a hint of sage. Complements roast pork, poultry stuffing, curries, vegetables, pickles, lentils, Middle Eastern dishes, chutney, stewed fruit, cakes and biscuits.

Dill Seed
Similar to caraway in flavor. Complements pickles, soups, salads (cucumber, potato, coleslaw), sauces, meats and fish, sauerkraut or boiled cabbage. For an interesting flavor, add a few seeds to an apple pie.

Fennel Seed
Subtle, sweet anise-like flavor. Complements eggs, cheese, apples, pickles, rice, veal, pork, fish and potatoes/potato salad.

Part 2

Cooking with Fresh Herbs

What a great place to start off a wonderful meal or gathering—by introducing the taste of fresh herbs in the first few bites! Herbs arouse the senses and get the appetite going. There are lots of recipes in this chapter, from amazing dips and spreads to sumptuous hors d'oeuvres that you can pop right into your mouth. It's worth hosting a cocktail party just so you can serve these delightful savory morsels.

APPETIZERS

Recipes

Baked Brie with Pesto and Pine Nuts

This is an easy and elegant appetizer combining rich, smooth Brie and aromatic pesto.

1	round (4 oz/125 g) Brie cheese	1
2 tbsp	Basil Pesto (see page 141)	30 mL
1 tbsp	pine nuts	15 mL

1. Using a sharp knife, cut white rind off top of Brie, leaving sides and bottom intact. Place Brie cut side up in a glass pie plate or small baking pan.
2. Spread pesto over top of Brie; sprinkle with pine nuts.
3. Bake in a 400°F (200°C) oven for 8 to 10 minutes or until heated through. (Or microwave on high for 1 to 2 minutes.) Serve immediately with assorted crackers.

Makes about 4 servings.

Variation

Use walnuts to make pesto then top with 1/4 cup (60 mL) chopped walnuts. (Walnuts from California have the freshest flavor.)

Tomato Bruschetta

Pronounced "bru-sketa," this popular restaurant appetizer is a cinch to make at home. Make sure to add it to the menu in mid-summer when locally grown tomatoes and basil are in abundance.

1 lb	tomatoes (about 3 large)	500 g
3 tbsp	finely chopped fresh basil	45 mL
2 tbsp	finely chopped red onions or shallots	30 mL
1 tbsp	olive oil	15 mL
1	clove garlic, minced or crushed	1
	Salt and pepper	
8	slices thick crusty Italian bread	8

1. Halve tomatoes; squeeze out seeds and juice. Dice and place in bowl.
2. Stir in basil, onion, oil, garlic, and a little salt and pepper. Let stand at room temperature for one hour. Taste and adjust seasoning.
3. Toast bread on both sides under broiler. Spoon tomato mixture on top and serve immediately.

Makes 4 servings.

tip

Add a pinch of granulated sugar to tomato mixture when tomatoes are out of season.

Mushroom Bruschetta

Here's a twist on popular tomato bruschetta for mushroom lovers! You can use your favorite mix of cultivated wild mushrooms. Serve as a party appetizer or with the salad course.

8 oz	mushrooms (button or cremini), coarsely chopped 250 g
1/2 cup	chopped green onions 125 mL
1/2 cup	grated Parmesan cheese 125 mL
1/4 cup	finely chopped fresh parsley 60 mL
2 tsp	finely chopped fresh thyme or lemon thyme 10 mL
3 tbsp	olive oil 45 mL
1 tbsp	balsamic or red wine vinegar 15 mL
1	baguette or French stick, about 18 inches (45 cm) long 1

1. In a medium bowl, mix together mushrooms, green onions, cheese, parsley, thyme, 2 tbsp (30 mL) of the oil and vinegar.
2. Slice bread into slices 1/2 inch (1 cm) thick. Brush tops with the remaining 1 tbsp (15 mL) of the oil; toast under broiler until golden.
3. Top with mushroom mixture; broil until hot and bubbling. Serve hot.

Makes 6 servings.

Creamy Chive and Garlic Dip

To serve this dip as a spread, decrease sour cream to 1/4 cup (60 mL). If dip is too thick, add more sour cream to reach desired consistency. You may omit the garlic and substitute chives with 2 tbsp (30 mL) garlic chives. Garnish with chive florets if desired.

1	pkg (8 oz/250 g) cream cheese, softened 1
1/2 cup	sour cream or plain yogurt 125 mL
2	cloves garlic, minced 2
1/4 cup	chopped fresh chives 60 mL
1/4 cup	chopped fresh parsley 60 mL
	Pepper, to taste

1. In food processor, purée all ingredients until smooth. Chill for several hours to allow flavors to blend.
2. Serve with chopped raw vegetables or crackers.

Makes about 1 cup (250 mL).

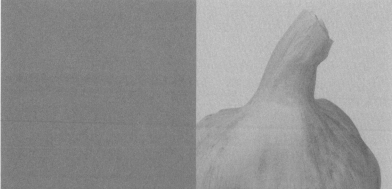

Classic Spinach Dip in a Pumpernickel Bowl

Serve this dip with assorted raw vegetables, such as carrot and celery sticks, broccoli and cauliflower florets, mushrooms, sweet pepper strips, etc.

1	pkg (10 oz/284 g) frozen chopped spinach thawed and well drained 1
1 cup	sour cream or plain yogurt 250 mL
1 cup	mayonnaise or creamy salad dressing 250 mL
1/2 cup	chopped fresh parsley 125 mL
1/4 cup	snipped fresh chives 60 mL
2 tbsp	chopped fresh dill 30 mL
2 tbsp	minced sweet red or yellow pepper 30 mL
1 tbsp	lemon juice 15 mL
1	round pumpernickel bread, unsliced 1

1. In a large bowl, mix together spinach, sour cream, mayonnaise, parsley, chives, dill, sweet pepper and lemon juice. Refrigerate for at least 1 hour to allow flavors to blend.
2. Slice top off bread; cut top into chunks. Remove center of bread in chunks, leaving a 1-inch (2.5 cm) thick crust to form bowl. Reserve bread chunks.
3. Just before serving, spoon dip into bread bowl. Place on serving platter; surround with bread chunks and raw vegetables.

Makes 10 to 12 servings.

Creamy Tuna Dip

This easy-to-make recipe can be doubled. Serve with carrot and celery sticks, sweet pepper and zucchini strips, and bread sticks.

1	can (6 oz/170 g) flaked white tuna, well drained 1
1	pkg (4 oz/125 g) cream cheese, softened 1
1 tbsp	minced onion 15 mL
1 tsp	lemon juice 5 mL
1/2 tsp	Worcestershire sauce 2 mL
1/2 tsp	minced garlic 2 mL
2 tbsp	mayonnaise 30 mL
2 tbsp	finely chopped fresh dill 30 mL

1. In food processor, place tuna, cream cheese, onion, lemon juice, Worcestershire sauce and garlic. Process until smooth, scraping down sides with spatula.
2. Add mayonnaise and dill; pulse until well combined. Refrigerate for up to two days.

Makes 1 cup (250 mL).

Variation
Use 1 tbsp (15 mL) finely chopped fresh savory in place of dill.

Guacamole

Serve guacamole as an accompaniment to Mexican dishes, such as tostadas, enchiladas, quesadillas and nachos.

3	ripe avocados 3
1	medium tomato, seeded and diced 1
1/4 cup	diced sweet onion 60 mL
1 tbsp	lime juice 15 mL
1 tbsp	minced jalapeño peppers 15 mL
1 tbsp	finely chopped fresh cilantro (or to taste) 15 mL
	Cilantro sprigs, for garnish

1. Pit and peel avocados; mash with fork until chunky or smooth, as desired.
2. Stir in remaining ingredients. Cover with plastic wrap; wrap should be directly on surface to avoid discoloration of avocado. Refrigerate until serving. Garnish with cilantro sprigs.

Makes about 2-1/2 cups (625 mL).

tip

To remove the pit from an avocado, slice lengthwise and twist to separate halves. Imbed knife blade in pit and twist to remove. If desired, imbed pit in guacamole to prevent browning.

Hot Salsa and Cheese Dip

This dip is great for warming up from the inside after cool-weather outdoor activities, whether it's touch football, skating, skiing, tobogganing or a brisk walk.

1	pkg (8 oz/250 g) cream cheese 1
1 cup	18% cream 250 mL
1 cup	commercial salsa 250 mL
1 cup	shredded Monterey Jack cheese 250 mL
2 tbsp	chopped fresh cilantro 30 mL
1 tbsp	snipped fresh chives 15 mL
	Taco chips

1. In a small saucepan over medium heat, place cream cheese, cream and salsa. Heat, stirring constantly, until cream cheese melts and all ingredients are blended.
2. Add Monterey Jack cheese; stir until smooth.
3. Remove from heat; stir in cilantro and chives. Serve warm with taco chips.

Makes 4 to 6 servings.

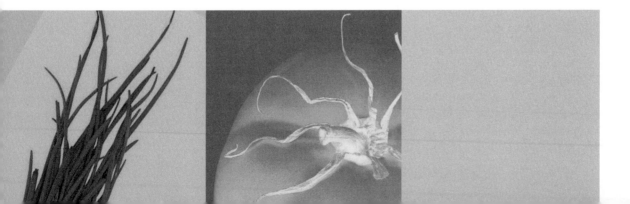

Salsa Dip

Serve this dip with corn tortilla chips, spoon it over baked potatoes, use it as a dip for cooked shrimp or serve it with quesadillas.

1	pkg (4 oz/125 g) cream cheese, softened 1
1/2 cup	sour cream 125 mL
1/2 cup	salsa (store-bought or homemade, mild or hot) 125 mL
1/4 cup	chopped fresh cilantro 60 mL

1. Using electric mixer, beat cream cheese until smooth. Beat in sour cream.
2. Stir in salsa and cilantro.

Makes about 1-1/2 cups (375 mL).

Zesty Bean Dip or Spread

Beans are an excellent source of fiber. This hummus-like dip/spread is lower in fat than recipes that use tahini (sesame-seed paste). It can be scooped up with crackers or dipped into with raw vegetables or Tortilla Crisps (recipe follows). To make a thinner dip, stir in about 1/4 cup (60 mL) plain low-fat yogurt.

2	cloves garlic	2
1	can (19 oz/540 mL) white kidney beans, drained and rinsed	1
1 tbsp	olive oil	15 mL
1 tbsp	finely chopped fresh savory or dill	15 mL
1 tbsp	lemon juice	15 mL
1/4 tsp	each: salt, ground cumin, paprika	1 mL
	Paprika and chopped fresh parsley, for garnish	
	Tortilla Crisps (recipe follows)	

1. In food processor, mince garlic. Add beans, oil, savory, lemon juice, salt, cumin and paprika; process until smooth. (For thinner dipping consistency, blend in a bit of water.)
2. Spread onto a large plate (or spoon into a shallow bowl). Sprinkle top lightly with paprika; add parsley around edge to garnish.
3. Serve at room temperature. (May be made ahead and refrigerated up to 48 hours.)

Makes 1-1/2 cups (375 mL).

Variations

- Substitute white pea beans, black beans or chick-peas for the white kidney beans (which are sometimes labeled cannellini beans).
- Use fresh basil in place of savory; top with chopped sun-dried tomatoes and toasted pine nuts.
- For extra heat, add minced jalapeños, hot pepper sauce or cayenne pepper.
- Substitute chopped fresh coriander for the parsley.

Tortilla Crisps

4	large flour tortillas (any type)	4
2 tsp	(approx.) olive oil	10 mL

1. Lightly brush both sides of each tortilla with a little olive oil. Cut each tortilla into 8 wedges; place in a single layer on a baking sheet.
2. Bake in a 375°F (190°C) oven for 6 to 8 minutes, turning once, until crisp. Let cool. If desired, store in tightly covered container up to 24 hours. Re-crisp in warm oven if necessary.

Makes 32 pieces.

Cheddar Chive Spread

I developed this spread for crackers and soon discovered that it is terrific as a baked potato topping and as an alternative to cheese sauce on boiled cauliflower or broccoli. It's a "cheese and celery sticks" spread for grown-ups.

1-1/2 cups	shredded sharp (old) Cheddar cheese 375 mL
1/4 cup	butter, softened 60 mL
1/2 tsp	Dijon mustard 2 mL
1 tbsp	finely chopped fresh chives 15 mL

1. In food processor, blend all ingredients until smooth. Keeps in refrigerator for up to a week.

Makes about 3/4 cup (175 mL).

Greek Red Pepper and Feta Spread

This spread has a rich satisfying flavor. Use to stuff chicken breasts.

2 tbsp	olive oil	30 mL
1	large sweet red pepper, chopped	1
1/4 tsp	hot red pepper flakes	1 mL
2 tsp	chopped fresh thyme or marjoram	10 mL
8 oz	feta cheese, crumbled	250 g

1. In a large skillet over medium heat, heat oil. Add sweet pepper and pepper flakes. Cook, stirring often, until peppers are very soft, about 10 minutes.

2. Stir in thyme; cook for 1 minute. Remove from heat; let cool.

3. Scrape pepper/oil mixture from skillet into bowl of food processor; add feta. Pulse on and off until smooth. Transfer to serving bowl. Store, covered, in refrigerator up to a week. Bring to room temperature for serving. Serve with crackers or pita triangles.

Makes about 1-1/3 cups (325 mL).

Herbed Chèvre Spread

This tasty spread was a hit at my herb cooking classes. Try it stuffed in blanched snow pea pods as an interesting appetizer.

1-1/4 cups	chèvre cheese (at room temperature) 300 mL
1/2 cup	ricotta cheese 125 mL
2	cloves garlic, minced 2
1/4 cup	chopped fresh parsley 60 mL
2 tbsp	chopped fresh basil 30 mL
2 tbsp	chopped fresh tarragon 30 mL
	Pepper, to taste
pinch	cayenne pepper, optional pinch

1. In a medium bowl, mix together chèvre, ricotta and garlic until smooth.
2. Stir in parsley, basil and tarragon; season with pepper; refrigerate for about 1 hour. To serve, bring to room temperature.

Makes about 2 cups (500 mL).

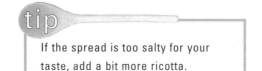

tip

If the spread is too salty for your taste, add a bit more ricotta.

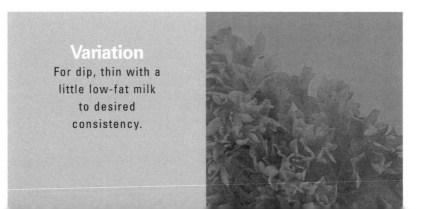

Variation
For dip, thin with a little low-fat milk to desired consistency.

Herbed Cream Cheese

This is similar to Boursin and Rondele brands of herb spreads. It's great on bagels and crackers or with crusty bread, olives, sliced Italian salami and raw vegetables. Other ideas for using this spread: in scrambled eggs; on baked potatoes; as a stuffing for cherry tomatoes or blanched pea pods; stuffed into mushroom caps and baked; stirred into warmed heavy cream and sprinkled with Parmesan cheese as a sauce for pasta; as a spread for roast beef, chicken or turkey sandwiches.

1	pkg (8 oz/250 g) cream cheese, softened 1
2 tbsp	soft butter 30 mL
1 or 2	cloves garlic, crushed (see page 144 about crushed garlic) 1 or 2
	Herb Mix (see below)
	Coarsely ground pepper, optional

1. In food processor, place cream cheese, butter and garlic; process until smooth. (May also be beaten with electric mixer in medium bowl.)
2. Add a herb mix; pulse several times until well mixed, scraping down sides. (If making in a bowl, stir in herbs.) Season with pepper (if using).
3. Refrigerate for several hours to blend flavors. Let rest at room temperature for about 30 minutes to soften to spreadable consistency. To store, refrigerate for up to 5 days or freeze for up to 3 months.

Makes 1 cup (250 mL).

Variations
Herb Mixes
• 1 tbsp (15 mL) each: finely chopped fresh basil, chives and dill
• 1 tbsp (15 mL) each: finely chopped fresh basil, parsley and oregano or marjoram
• 1 tbsp (15 mL) each: finely chopped fresh lemon thyme, oregano and parsley
• 2 tbsp (30 mL) finely chopped fresh parsley or chervil and 1 tbsp (15 mL) finely chopped fresh chives
• 1 tbsp (15 mL) each: finely chopped fresh parsley and chives, and 2 tsp (10 mL) each: finely chopped fresh chervil and tarragon

Other Variations
• Omit butter; mix in 2 tbsp (30 mL) (or to taste) Olive and Sun-Dried Tomato Tapenade (see page 64) or Basil Pesto (see page 141).
• Use 1/2 tsp (2 mL) Herbes de Provence, 1 tbsp (15 mL) finely chopped fresh parsley and 1 tsp (5 mL) red wine vinegar.
• Mix 1 tbsp (15 mL) finely chopped fresh dill and 1 tsp (5 mL) lemon juice, and add to cream cheese; serve on bagels or pumpernickel bread with smoked salmon, topped with thinly sliced sweet onion and capers.

Herb-Marinated Goat Cheese

Chèvre is a smooth goat cheese from France, but very good locally made renditions are quite delicious too. Herbs and garlic are a wonderful accent to its tangy flavor. Serve with crusty French bread (and a glass of French wine!) for an appetizer or snack.

1	pkg (8 oz/250 g) chèvre 1
1/2 cup	olive oil (or Herb Oil, see page 25) 125 mL
1/4 cup	chopped fresh basil 60 mL
2 tsp	minced fresh rosemary, oregano or marjoram 10 mL
1 tsp	minced fresh thyme or lemon thyme 5 mL
1	clove garlic, minced 1
1/4 tsp	coarsely ground black pepper 1 mL

1. Place cheese log in freezer for about 30 minutes to make firm for easier slicing. Slice into 1/2-inch (1 cm) thick rounds. Place in shallow baking dish in single layer.
2. In a small bowl, whisk together oil, basil, rosemary, thyme, garlic and pepper. Pour over cheese; turn cheese to coat on both sides. Cover and refrigerate for at least 8 hours or overnight. Store for up to 1 week in refrigerator. Bring to room temperature before serving.

Makes 4 to 6 servings.

tip

Use dental floss or fishing line to slice cheese. Stretch floss between your hands and press down on cheese log to make a clean round slice.

Variations

- Use 1 tbsp (15 mL) Herbes de Provence (see page 3) instead of the fresh herbs. Add 1 tsp (5 mL) lemon juice.
- In a small saucepan over medium-high heat, heat oil, garlic, 6 whole peppercorns, 1 bay leaf and a pinch of hot red pepper flakes just until mixture bubbles. Remove from heat; stir in herbs and let cool. Pour over cheese.
- **Marinated Feta Cheese:** Use 1/2-inch (1 cm) cubes of feta cheese instead of chèvre.
- Place cheese rounds on toasted French stick bread rounds. Place on baking sheet under broiler about 6 inches (15 cm) from heat until golden brown and bubbling.

Marinated Mushrooms

These mushrooms make a tasty addition to an antipasto platter or as an appetizer at a barbecue. To serve as a side salad, use larger mushrooms and thinly slice them or cut them into quarters.

1 lb	small button mushrooms (about 1-inch/2.5 cm diameter) 500 g
1/4 cup	oil 60 mL
2 tbsp	lemon juice 30 mL
1/4 tsp	salt 1 mL
2 tbsp	finely chopped fresh parsley 30 mL
1 tbsp	finely chopped chives 15 mL
1 tsp	finely chopped fresh thyme or lemon thyme 5 mL
	Pepper, to taste

1. Wash mushrooms well; trim stems.
2. In a large bowl, whisk together oil, lemon juice, salt, parsley, chives, thyme and a few grinds of pepper.
3. Add mushrooms; toss to coat well. Cover and refrigerate for 1 hour.

Makes 4 servings.

Mini Greek-Style Lamb Burgers

I call these mini burgers "lamb-burg-inis"; they are great to serve at a barbecue buffet. Look for ground lamb in your supermarket, or ask your butcher to grind a fresh boneless lamb shoulder for you.

1 lb	ground lamb 500 g
1/3 cup	dry breadcrumbs 75 mL
1	egg, beaten 1
1/4 cup	grated onion (1 small) 60 mL
1/4 cup	each: chopped fresh parsley and mint 60 mL
1/2 tsp	cinnamon 2 mL
1/2 tsp	salt 2 mL
1/4 tsp	black pepper 1 mL
1	clove garlic, minced, optional 1
20	mini pitas 20 (or five 7-inch pitas, cut into quarters)
	Tzatziki (see page 144)

1. In a medium bowl, break up lamb using the back of a wooden spoon. Add breadcrumbs, egg, onion, parsley, mint, cinnamon, salt, pepper and garlic (if using; you may want to omit garlic if serving burgers with tzatziki). Stir until well combined.

2. Form mixture into 20 meatballs; flatten to form 1/2-inch (1 cm) thick patties. If not cooking immediately, arrange on a platter with waxed paper between layers; refrigerate, covered, for up to 4 hours.

3. Preheat barbecue. Place burgers on oiled barbecue grill; grill over medium-high heat with lid closed for about 10 minutes, turning once halfway through cooking, until burgers are no longer pink inside.

4. With sharp knife, slit open each mini pita or pita quarter to make pocket. Place a burger and a spoonful of tzatziki in each pocket.

Makes 20.

Rosemary and Thyme Marinated Olives

In the Mediterranean, olives are set out as appetizers in bowls, or served with a lunch of bread and cheese or fruit. Use a variety of olives such as green or Kalamata.

1/4 cup	extra-virgin olive oil	60 mL
2 tbsp	fresh lemon juice	30 mL
4	cloves garlic, cut into slivers	4
4 tbsp	chopped fresh rosemary	60 mL
1 tbsp	chopped fresh thyme	15 mL
	Pepper, to taste	
4 cups	mixed olives	1 L

1. In a large bowl, whisk together olive oil and lemon juice. Stir in garlic, rosemary, thyme and pepper. Stir in olives. Refrigerate for 1 or 2 days to blend flavors, stirring a few times.
2. Serve with pita, French, Italian or other bread. Can be stored in the refrigerator for several weeks.

Makes 4 cups (1L).

tip

Give a jar of these olives as a host/hostess gift. Place a few fresh sprigs of rosemary on the inside of the jar against the glass.

Simon's Famous Stuffed Mushroom Caps

My brother's friend in London, England (hence the Stilton cheese), served these as a starter to an elegant English dinner. I could easily have eaten two!

4	portobello mushrooms 4
	Olive oil
2	slices bacon, diced 2
1/4 cup	finely chopped onion or shallots 60 mL
1	clove garlic, minced 1
1 tsp	finely chopped thyme, lemon thyme or rosemary 5 mL (or 1/4 tsp/1 mL Herbes de Provence, see page 3)
2 tbsp	grated Parmesan cheese 30 mL
2 tbsp	finely chopped fresh parsley 30 mL
4 oz	Stilton cheese 125 g
2 oz	Parmesan cheese, in shavings or thinly sliced 60 g

1. Wipe mushrooms clean with a damp paper towel. Trim stem ends, then remove stems from caps with knife; finely chop stems and set aside. Brush outside of caps with a little oil and place top down on a baking sheet; set aside.

2. In a large skillet over medium heat, cook bacon, onion and garlic for about 3 minutes, until bacon is partially cooked. Stir in chopped mushroom stems and thyme; cook until onion and mushrooms are soft. Stir in the grated Parmesan cheese and parsley.

3. Fill mushroom caps with filling, top each with a slice of Stilton and the shavings or thin slices of Parmesan cheese.

4. Bake in a 400°F (200°C) oven for 10 to 12 minutes until caps are tender and cheese melts. Serve immediately.

Makes 4 servings.

Olive and Sun-Dried Tomato Tapenade

This tasty spread from Provence, in southern France, derives its name from the French word for capers. For an *olivada*, omit capers and sun-dried tomatoes; use lemon juice in place of balsamic vinegar.

1 cup	pitted Kalamata olives	250 mL
1/4 cup	chopped sun-dried tomatoes	60 mL
1 or 2	cloves garlic	1 or 2
2 tbsp	olive oil	30 mL
2 tbsp	finely chopped fresh curly or Italian parsley	30 mL
1 tbsp	capers, optional	15 mL
2 tsp	finely chopped fresh rosemary	10 mL
1 tsp	finely chopped fresh thyme or lemon thyme	5 mL
1 tsp	balsamic vinegar	5 mL
	Pepper, to taste	

1. In food processor, place all ingredients. Pulse on and off until almost smooth.
2. Transfer to a serving bowl. Let rest at room temperature for about an hour to let flavors develop. Serve at room temperature with crackers or Crostini (recipe follows). To store, cover surface with thin layer of olive oil and plastic wrap; refrigerate for up to 2 weeks.

Makes 1 cup (250 mL).

Crostini (little toasts)

Slice a baguette or French stick into 1/2-inch (1 cm) thick rounds. Arrange on a baking sheet. Bake in a 350°F (180°C) oven for about 8 minutes on each side, until golden brown. While still warm, rub one side of each toast with a cut clove of garlic, then brush with a little olive oil. (If making ahead, store in an airtight container overnight at room temperature. Re-crisp in a 350°F/180°C oven for a few minutes before serving.)

tip

Stir together equal amounts of tapenade and mayonnaise and serve with hard-cooked eggs, tomatoes, chicken, turkey or fish.

Basil Pesto Torte

Bring this to your next party or make it for guests—they'll all want the recipe! Strictly for basil lovers.

1	pkg (8 oz/250 g) cream cheese, softened 1
8 oz	chèvre (goat cheese), softened 250 g
1/2 cup	butter, softened 125 mL
1 cup	Basil Pesto (see page 141) 250 mL
1/2 cup	toasted pine nuts 125 mL
1/2 cup	chopped sun-dried tomatoes 125 mL
	Basil leaves, for garnish

1. In food processor or a bowl, mix together cream cheese, chèvre and butter until well blended.
2. In a 7- or 8-inch (18 or 20 cm) springform pan, begin with a layer of one-third of the cheese mixture. Next spread half of the pesto, another one-third of the cheese mixture, the remaining pesto and the last layer of cheese. Refrigerate for at least 1 hour. (If you do not have a springform pan, line a small, straight-sided bowl or round casserole with plastic wrap. After chilling, invert torte onto a plate; remove plastic.)
3. Arrange pine nuts on top in a spoked wheel pattern; fill in between spokes with sun-dried tomatoes. Garnish center with fresh basil leaves. Remove sides of pan and serve torte with assorted crackers or melba toast. Allow to warm a bit before serving so that it is spreadable.

Makes 15 to 20 appetizer servings.

tip

• Chill cheese layers before spreading with pesto to get smoother layers.
• May be made several days ahead; top with toasted pine nuts and sun-dried tomatoes just before serving.

Smoked Salmon Terrine

My friend Rose brings this wonderful terrine to parties. There are never any leftovers and there are lots of requests for the recipe. Serve with rice crackers or small slices of pumpernickel bread.

1/4 cup	butter, softened 60 mL
1/4 cup	mayonnaise 60 mL
2	cloves garlic, minced 2
1/2 tsp	lemon juice 2 mL
1/4 tsp	each: salt and pepper 1 mL
1	can (7.5 oz/213 g) salmon 1
3 tbsp	each: finely chopped fresh dill and parsley 45 mL
2 tbsp	each: finely chopped fresh basil and chives 30 mL
4	slices smoked salmon (about 1/4 lb/125 g total) 4
	Dill sprigs and lemon slices, for garnish

1. In a medium bowl, mix together butter and mayonnaise. Add garlic, lemon juice, salt and pepper; mix well.
2. Drain salmon; remove skin and bones and flake with fork. Add salmon, dill, parsley, basil and chives to mayonnaise mixture; mix well.
3. Using kitchen scissors, snip one slice of smoked salmon into small bits; stir into canned salmon mixture. Repeat with other slices of smoked salmon.
4. Line a 2-cup (500 mL) bowl or mold with plastic wrap, leaving about 3 inches (7.5 cm) of wrap overhanging. If desired, place a sprig of dill in the bottom of the bowl. Pack mixture into bowl, flattening the surface. Refrigerate for at least 4 hours or up to 24 hours.
5. To serve, place plate over bowl; quickly turn plate and bowl over. Remove bowl and plastic wrap. If refrigerated for 24 hours, let stand at room temperature for 30 minutes before serving. Garnish plate with dill sprigs and lemon slices.

Makes 8 to 12 servings.

Mediterranean Tarts

This recipe has been adapted from the original, courtesy of the International Olive Oil Council. The flavorful vegetable filling for these tarts can be made a couple of days ahead. For speedy assembly, start with tiny pre-baked tart shells. If they are not available, make Toast Cups (recipe follows).

3 tbsp	olive oil 45 mL
1	large red onion, thinly sliced 1
2	cloves garlic, minced 2
1	each: sweet red and yellow pepper, thinly sliced 1
	Salt and pepper
1 tsp	each: minced fresh oregano, rosemary and thyme 5 mL
1/3 cup	slivered fresh basil 75 mL
2 tbsp	minced fresh parsley 30 mL
1/4 cup	coarsely chopped pitted Kalamata olives 60 mL
36	small baked tart shells (1-1/2-inch/4 cm rounds) 36
	Small sprigs of fresh oregano, for garnish

1. In a large skillet over medium heat, heat oil. Add onion, garlic and sweet peppers. Season with a little salt and pepper. Cook, stirring often, for about 30 minutes until onions and peppers are very soft.

2. Stir in oregano, rosemary and thyme; cook for 5 minutes longer.

3. Stir in basil and parsley; cook for 2 minutes longer. Remove from heat and stir in olives. Taste and adjust seasoning. (Mixture can be prepared up to 2 days ahead; keep refrigerated. Bring to room temperature to serve.)

4. To serve, spoon room-temperature mixture into tart shells or toast cups; garnish with oregano sprigs.

Makes 3 dozen.

Toast Cups

Cut crusts from 9 thin slices of white bread. Using a rolling pin, roll out bread flat; cut each slice into quarters. Press into greased mini-tart tins. (Or roll out enough bread to cut into rounds with a cookie cutter to fit mini-tart tins.) Brush lightly with olive oil. Bake in a 350°F (180°C) oven for 5 to 7 minutes, or until crisp and golden. Let cool before filling. (Can be stored in an airtight container for several days.)

Tomato Tarts

Two great summer tastes—local-grown or home-grown tomatoes and fresh herbs! For appetizers, cut each tart into four squares or triangles after baking.

2 tbsp	finely chopped fresh basil 30 mL
1 tbsp	finely chopped fresh marjoram 15 mL
2 tsp	olive oil 10 mL
1/2 tsp	crushed garlic 2 mL
1	pkg (411 or 397 g) puff pastry, thawed according to package directions 1
4	medium tomatoes, sliced very thinly 4
	Pepper, to taste
1/3 cup	crumbled chèvre or freshly grated Parmesan cheese 75 mL

1. In a small bowl, mix together basil, marjoram, oil and garlic. Let stand.
2. On a floured surface, roll out each half of the pastry to a 9-inch (23 cm) square. Cut each into four 4-1/2-inch (11 cm) squares, to make 8 squares. Place on a large baking sheet.
3. Stir herb mixture and spread evenly over pastry squares. Top with tomato slices (about 3 per tart), overlapping slightly. Season with pepper and sprinkle with a little chèvre or Parmesan cheese.
4. Bake in a 400°F (200°C) oven for 20 to 25 minutes or until pastry is crisp and golden. Serve warm.

Makes 8 tarts or 32 appetizers.

Variation
Before baking, drizzle with balsamic vinegar and top with finely chopped sun-dried tomatoes or black olives.

Herbs can be used in a bouquet garni to flavor stock, cooked directly into the soup, added at the end of cooking or used to garnish the soup. A garnish may be as simple as a sprinkling of chopped fresh parsley, chiffonade of basil, blades or snips of chives, a sprig of dill, a swirl of pesto or pistou in vegetable soup, herbed croutons in a creamed soup or edible flowers floating on a chilled summer soup.

SOUPS

Recipes

Beef and Barley Soup

This is a hearty soup, ideal for meat and potato types. Serve with slices of whole grain bread for a delicious meal.

3 tbsp	oil 45 mL
1 lb	stewing beef or sirloin steak, cut into 1/2-inch (1 cm) pieces 500 g
1	medium onion, chopped 1
2	stalks celery, diced 2
1 cup	diced carrots 250 mL
1	large clove garlic, minced 1
8 cups	beef stock 2 L
1 lb	red-skinned potatoes (unpeeled), cut into 1/2-inch (1 cm) chunks 500 g
1/4 cup	pearl barley 60 mL
1	bay leaf 1
2 tsp	finely chopped fresh thyme 10 mL
2 tsp	Worcestershire sauce 10 mL
1/2 cup	chopped fresh parsley 125 mL
	Salt and pepper, to taste

1. In a large Dutch oven over medium-high heat, heat 2 tbsp (30 mL) of the oil. Add beef; cook, stirring, until liquid from meat has evaporated and meat is lightly browned. Remove beef to bowl using slotted spoon; set aside.

2. Add the remaining 1 tbsp (15 mL) of the oil to pot. Stir in onions, celery and carrots; reduce heat to medium and cook for 7 minutes, stirring occasionally. Stir in garlic; cook for 1 minute.

3. Stir in stock, potatoes, pearl barley and bay leaf. Increase heat to high and bring to a boil, stirring occasionally. Reduce heat, partially cover and simmer for 20 minutes.

4. Stir in thyme and Worcestershire sauce; cook for 10 minutes more.

5. Stir in parsley. Season with salt and pepper. Discard bay leaf.

Makes 6 servings.

Carrot, Orange and Thyme Soup

"Keep your cool" when you serve this delicious chilled soup. For a flavor switch, use fresh cilantro, dill, fennel, tarragon or lemon thyme.

3 tbsp	oil	45 mL
5 cups	sliced carrots	1.25 L
2	medium onions, sliced	2
4 cups	chicken or vegetable stock	1 L
2 tbsp	fresh thyme	30 mL
1	bay leaf	1
1 cup	orange juice	250 mL
	Salt and pepper, to taste	
	Yogurt, thyme sprigs, chopped fresh chives, chive florets or parsley, for garnish	

1. In a large saucepan over medium-low heat, heat oil. Stir in carrots and onions; cover and cook for 8 minutes, stirring occasionally.
2. Add stock, thyme and bay leaf. Increase heat to high and bring to a boil. Reduce heat; cover and simmer for 15 to 20 minutes or until carrots are tender. Discard bay leaf.
3. Using a slotted spoon, transfer vegetables to food processor or blender; purée with a little soup stock until smooth. Return to saucepan.
4. Stir in orange juice. Season with salt and pepper; chill for at least 1 hour. (May be made a day ahead and refrigerated.) If desired, serve in chilled glass bowl.
5. Garnish with a drizzle or dollop of yogurt and a sprig of thyme, or sprinkle with chopped chives, chive florets or parsley.

Makes 6 servings.

Cauliflower and Potato Soup

The fresh taste of the herbs really comes through when they are added just before serving. When chives are in flower, add a few florets to the herb mixture for added color.

2 tbsp	oil	30 mL
1	large onion, chopped	1
1/4 cup	diced celery, optional	60 mL
1	clove garlic, minced	1
2 cups	peeled, diced potatoes	500 mL
1	bay leaf	1
6 cups	chicken or vegetable stock	1.5 L
6 cups	cauliflower florets	1.5 L
1 cup	diced carrots	250 mL
	Salt and pepper, to taste	
2 tbsp	each: finely chopped fresh chives, dill and parsley	30 mL

1. In a Dutch oven or large saucepan over medium heat, heat oil. Add onions and celery (if using); cook for 7 minutes or until softened.
2. Add garlic, potatoes and bay leaf; cook, stirring, for about 2 minutes.
3. Stir in stock, cauliflower and carrots; increase heat to high and bring to a boil. Reduce heat; simmer for about 10 minutes or until all vegetables are tender.
4. Remove bay leaf. Remove about 3 cups (750 mL) of the vegetables and a small amount of the soup stock. In food processor or blender, purée until smooth. Stir back into soup. Season with salt and pepper.
5. In small bowl, mix together chives, dill and parsley. To serve, sprinkle each serving with mixed herbs.

Makes 6 to 8 servings.

Variation
Use purple basil or marjoram in place of dill.

Cool Cucumber Mint Soup

Serve this refreshing chilled soup as an appetizer or starter, topped with colorful chive blossoms. It has eye *and* appetite appeal, is low-fat and quick to prepare.

1	English cucumber, unpeeled	1
1	clove garlic	1
1 cup	chicken or vegetable stock, chilled	250 mL
1 cup	plain yogurt	250 mL
1/4 cup	chopped fresh mint	60 mL
1 tsp	lemon juice	5 mL
	Salt and pepper, to taste	
	Mint leaves, chopped fresh chives or chive flowers, for garnish	

1. Cut cucumber into chunks and place in food processor or blender with garlic; process until cucumber is well chopped.
2. Add stock, yogurt, mint and lemon juice; process until smooth. Season with salt and pepper. Chill for at least 3 hours. Serve chilled in a chilled glass or glass bowl; garnish with mint leaves, chopped chives or chive flowers.

Makes 4 servings.

tip
Soup may also be made with regular cucumber. Peel and remove seeds first.

Gazpacho

This cool summer soup is best made when tomatoes are in season and at their best. This dish has its origin in Andalusia in southern Spain. Gazpacho recipes often don't include breadcrumbs, but it is the secret ingredient that keeps the soup from separating. Choose some of the interesting toppings listed below to serve in small bowls with the soup. It's a fun starter to serve at parties.

3 cups	peeled, seeded chopped tomatoes 750 mL
1/2 cup	finely chopped sweet onions or shallots 125 mL
1	field cucumber, peeled and seeded 1
1	sweet green pepper, chopped 1
1	clove garlic, minced 1
3 tbsp	olive oil 45 mL
1 cup	soft fresh breadcrumbs 250 mL
3 tbsp	chopped fresh basil 45 mL
1 tbsp	lemon or lime juice 15 mL
2 tbsp	red wine vinegar 30 mL
1/2 tsp	Worcestershire sauce 2 mL
1/4 tsp	hot pepper sauce or cayenne pepper 1 mL
	Salt and pepper, to taste

Toppings: diced red onions, sliced green onions, chopped tomato, chopped sweet yellow pepper, chopped cucumber, chopped hard-boiled egg, Parsleyed Croutons (see page 95)

1. In blender or food processor, combine tomatoes, onions, cucumber, green pepper, garlic and olive oil; purée to desired consistency (chunky or smooth).
2. Add breadcrumbs, basil, lemon juice, vinegar, Worcestershire and hot pepper sauces. Pulse to blend in. Season with salt and pepper. If desired, add more hot pepper sauce.
3. Chill for at least 1 hour before serving to allow flavors to develop. Serve with small bowls of toppings.

Makes 4 to 6 servings.

Variation
Use fresh cilantro or dill in place of basil. Use herb vinegar (basil, tarragon, dill) in place of red wine vinegar.

Green Pea Soup with Mint

This soup has just a hint of mint to set off the fresh taste of the peas. It is great served hot or cold.

2 tbsp	butter	30 mL
1 tbsp	oil	15 mL
2 cups	chopped leeks, white and light green parts only	500 mL
1 cup	peeled, diced potato	250 mL
2 tbsp	all-purpose flour	30 mL
6 cups	chicken or vegetable stock	1.5 L
5 cups	fresh or frozen peas	1.25 L
1	bay leaf	1
2 tbsp	finely chopped fresh mint	30 mL

Whipping cream, sour cream or plain yogurt

Parsleyed Croutons (see page 95)

Fresh mint sprigs or chives, each about 3 inches/7.5 cm in length, for garnish

1. In a Dutch oven or large saucepan over medium heat, heat butter and oil until butter foams. Stir in leeks; cook, stirring, for 5 minutes.
2. Stir in potatoes; cook for 3 minutes.
3. Stir in flour; cook for 2 minutes, stirring often.
4. Stir in stock, peas and bay leaf. Increase heat to high and bring to a boil. Reduce heat; cover and simmer for 15 minutes.
5. Remove bay leaf; stir in mint.
6. In food processor, purée in batches until smooth. If serving hot, return to pot and heat through. Serve with a drizzle of whipping cream and croutons. If serving cold, refrigerate for at least 1 hour and serve with a dollop of sour cream or yogurt. Garnish with mint sprigs or chives.

Makes 6 to 8 servings.

Variation
Use chervil instead of mint.

Minestrone

Here's a quick and hearty vegetable soup with a touch of herbs.
Serve with thick slices of whole grain bread for a satisfying dinner.

2 tbsp	olive oil	30 mL
1	large onion, chopped	1
2	cloves garlic, minced	2
1	medium zucchini, quartered lengthwise and sliced	1
6 cups	chicken or vegetable stock	1.5 L
1	can (19 oz/540 mL) diced tomatoes	1
1	can (19 oz/540 mL) mixed beans, drained and rinsed (or 2 cups/500 mL cooked beans, such as Romano, chick-peas, red or white kidney beans)	1
2 cups	frozen cut green beans	500 mL
1/2 tsp	dried oregano	2 mL
1/3 cup	orzo or small soup pasta	75 mL
1/3 cup	each: chopped fresh basil and parsley	75 mL
	Salt and pepper, to taste	
6 tbsp	grated Parmesan cheese	90 mL

1. In a large saucepan or Dutch oven over medium heat, heat oil. Add onion and cook, stirring often, for 7 minutes or until softened.
2. Stir in garlic and zucchini; cook, stirring often, for 3 minutes.
3. Stir in stock, tomatoes, mixed beans, green beans and oregano. Increase heat to high and bring to a boil. Reduce heat and simmer for 10 minutes.
4. Stir in orzo; simmer 5 minutes. Stir in basil and parsley. Season with salt and pepper.
5. Sprinkle 1 tbsp (15 mL) Parmesan cheese over each serving.

Makes 6 servings.

Squash and Sweet Potato Chowder

Here's a great soup to warm up with on chilly fall days. If desired, drizzle with a little sage oil (see page 25 for making herb oils) before serving.

2 tbsp	vegetable oil 30 mL
1	large onion, chopped 1
1	clove garlic, minced 1
3 cups	diced peeled sweet potatoes or potatoes 750 mL
3 cups	chicken or vegetable stock 750 mL
1 tsp	chopped fresh thyme 5 mL
1	fresh or dried bay leaf 1
2 cups	cooked mashed butternut squash or pumpkin 500 mL (or 14 oz/ 398 mL canned pumpkin)
1/2 cup	beer or milk 125 mL
1/4 tsp	salt 1 mL
	Pepper, to taste
	Snipped fresh chives
	Parsleyed Croutons (see page 95)
	or Fried Sage Leaves (see page 124), for garnish

1. In a large saucepan over medium heat, heat oil. Stir in onion, garlic and potatoes. Cook until onions are soft, stirring occasionally.
2. Add stock, thyme and bay leaf. Increase heat to high and bring to a boil. Reduce heat; cover and simmer 7 minutes or until potatoes are soft.
3. Stir in squash, beer and salt; season with pepper. In blender or food processor, purée soup until smooth. Heat through and serve garnished with chives, Parsleyed Croutons or Fried Sage Leaves.

Makes 4 to 6 servings.

Tortellini Soup

Buy ready-made frozen tortellini to have on hand for this soup. It's quick to make and makes a delicious meal served with a loaf of fresh Italian bread—*mange!*

2 tbsp	olive oil 30 mL
1	medium onion, chopped 1
1 cup	chopped carrots 250 mL
2 cups	chopped zucchini 500 mL
1/2 cup	diced green pepper 125 mL
1	can (28 oz/796 mL) tomatoes 1
2	cans each (10 oz/284 mL) chicken or vegetable stock 2
2 cups	frozen tortellini (meat- or cheese-filled) 500 mL
1/2 cup	chopped fresh parsley 125 mL
1/4 cup	chopped fresh basil 60 mL
	Grated Parmesan cheese, to taste

1. In a large saucepan over medium heat, heat oil. Add onion and carrots; cook for 7 minutes or until carrots are softened.
2. Add zucchini and green pepper; cook for 3 minutes.
3. Add tomatoes (with juice) and stock. Increase heat to high; bring to a boil.
4. Stir in tortellini; reduce heat and simmer for 15 to 18 minutes or until tortellini are tender (take one out to test).
5. Stir in parsley and basil. Pour into serving bowls; sprinkle with Parmesan cheese.

Makes 8 servings.

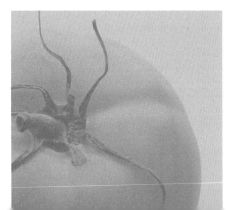

Wild Mushroom Soup with Thyme

Dried wild mushrooms are easy to find in supermarkets nowadays. They come packaged as individual types as well as mixed. This soup has a rich, earthy taste, sure to be savored by mushroom aficionados.

1 oz	mixed dried mushrooms (such as porcini, chanterelle, morel) 30 g
1/4 cup	butter 50 mL
2	medium onions, chopped 2
1	small clove garlic, minced 1
3 tbsp	all-purpose flour 45 mL
1 lb	sliced fresh mushrooms 500 g
5 cups	chicken or vegetable stock 1.25 L
1 tbsp	finely chopped fresh thyme 15 mL
1 cup	whipping cream (35%) 250 mL
	Salt and pepper, to taste
2 tbsp	finely chopped fresh parsley 30 mL
	Thinly sliced mushrooms or Parsleyed Croutons (see page 95), for garnish

1. Trim any tough stems from the dried mushrooms. Rinse and soak dried mushrooms in hot water for 30 minutes. Drain, reserving liquid; chop mushrooms.

2. In a large saucepan over low heat, melt butter. Add onions; cover and cook for 10 to 12 minutes or until very tender and golden.

3. Add garlic; cook for 2 minutes. Stir in flour; cook for 1 minute.

4. Stir in dried mushrooms and reserved liquid, fresh mushrooms, stock and thyme. Increase heat to high; bring to a boil. Reduce heat; cover and simmer for 40 minutes or until mushrooms are tender.

5. Strain soup, reserving 3 cups (750 mL) of liquid. Purée soup until smooth. Return purée and reserved liquid to saucepan. Stir in cream; season with salt and pepper. Garnish with parsley and thinly sliced mushrooms, or with Parsleyed Croutons.

Makes 4 servings.

Zesty Tomato and Dill Soup

When local tomatoes are abundant, make this soup using 3 cups (750 mL) chopped tomatoes and increase stock to 2 cups (500 mL).

1 tbsp	oil or butter	15 mL
1	medium onion, chopped	1
1	clove garlic, minced	1
1	can (28 oz/796 mL) diced tomatoes	1
1 cup	chicken or vegetable stock	250 mL
1/2 cup	commercial chili sauce	125 mL
1 tsp	brown sugar	5 mL
1/2 tsp	hot pepper sauce, or to taste	2 mL
2 tbsp	finely chopped fresh dill	30 mL
	Pepper, to taste	
4 tbsp	sour cream	60 mL
	Dill sprigs, for garnish	

1. In a large saucepan over medium heat, heat oil. Stir in onion; cook for 7 minutes or until soft. Stir in garlic; cook for 1 minute more.
2. Stir in tomatoes, stock, chili sauce, sugar and hot pepper sauce. Increase heat to high; bring to a boil. Reduce heat; cover and simmer for 10 minutes.
3. Stir in fresh dill and season with pepper. Remove about 2 cups (500 mL) of soup and purée in blender or food processor until smooth; stir back into soup.
4. Serve soup hot with 1 tbsp (15 mL) of sour cream in the center of each serving; garnish with a small sprig of dill.

Makes 4 servings.

Variation
Use fresh basil in place of dill; garnish with basil sprig.

Zucchini Basil Soup

This soup is a favorite to make in the summer when zucchini and fresh basil are both plentiful, but it is enjoyable year-round.

1 tbsp	oil	15 mL
1	medium onion, chopped	1
2	cloves garlic, minced	2
5	medium zucchini, chopped	5
4 cups	chicken or vegetable stock	1 L
1 tbsp	lemon juice	15 mL
2 tsp	granulated sugar	10 mL
1/3 cup	chopped fresh basil	75 mL
4 tbsp	plain yogurt or sour cream	60 mL
	Basil sprigs and paprika, for garnish	

1. In a large saucepan or Dutch oven over medium heat, heat oil. Add onion and cook, stirring often, for 7 minutes or until softened.
2. Add garlic and zucchini; cook, stirring occasionally, for 3 minutes.
3. Stir in stock, lemon juice and sugar. Increase heat to high; bring to a boil. Reduce heat and simmer, uncovered, for about 15 minutes, or until zucchini is tender. Stir in basil; simmer for 1 minute longer.
4. In blender or food processor, purée soup in small batches until smooth. Return to saucepan to heat through.
5. Spoon into serving bowls. Add 1 tbsp (15 mL) of yogurt in the center of each serving; garnish with a sprig of basil and a sprinkle of paprika.

Makes 4 servings.

tip

Use food processor to shred zucchini and save preparation and cooking time.

Herbs are eaten fresh in salads, either as an ingredient in the salad itself or to flavor the dressing. Salads range from fresh leafy greens to crisp colorful vegetables, from bread and pasta salads to mixtures of hearty grains and legumes, and can be served as appetizers or main courses. Edible flowers and herb flowers can be used to accent visual appeal.

SALADS AND DRESSINGS

Recipes

Baked Herbed Chèvre Salad

This is a delicious starter salad, topped with warm cheese rounds.

Herb Marinated Goat Cheese
(see page 59)

1/3 cup   fine dry breadcrumbs 75 mL

8 cups   mixed salad greens (mesclun):
radicchio, watercress, arugula,
endive, etc. 2 L

Chive flower blossoms,
optional

Vinaigrette (recipe follows)

1. Lift cheese from marinade and coat well in breadcrumbs, pressing to coat on both sides. Transfer cheese rounds to baking sheet; bake in a 425°F (220°C) oven for 4 to 6 minutes, or until cheese softens and crumbs are golden.
2. Place about 2 cups (500 mL) salad greens on each of four individual plates. Top with cheese rounds. Sprinkle with chive flowers (if using). Drizzle with Vinaigrette and serve immediately.

Makes 4 servings.

Vinaigrette

1/3 cup   olive oil 75 mL

2 tbsp   red wine or herb vinegar 30 mL

1 tsp   Dijon mustard 5 mL

1 tsp   granulated sugar 5 mL

1/2 tsp   paprika 2 mL

1   clove garlic, minced 1

          Pepper, to taste

1. Whisk together all ingredients.

Makes 3/4 cup (175 mL).

Bean Salad

Ever-popular bean salad is especially nice in the summer made with garden-fresh beans. It's commonly made with kidney beans, but these can be replaced with other types of beans or legumes, such as Romano or cannellini beans, chick-peas or mixed beans.

1/3 cup	olive oil 75 mL
2 tbsp	red wine or cider vinegar 30 mL
1 tsp	granulated sugar 5 mL
1 tsp	lemon juice 5 mL
1	clove garlic, crushed 1
	Hot pepper sauce, to taste
	Salt and pepper, to taste
1 lb	crisp-cooked green beans (or half green and half yellow beans), chopped 500 g
1	can (19 oz/540 mL) kidney beans, drained and rinsed 1
1/2 cup	chopped sweet yellow or red pepper 125 mL
1/2 cup	chopped red onion 125 mL
1 tbsp	finely chopped fresh savory 15 mL

1. In a small bowl, whisk together oil, vinegar, sugar, lemon juice, garlic, hot pepper sauce and a little salt and pepper; set aside.
2. In a large bowl, mix together green beans, kidney beans, sweet pepper, onion and savory. Pour dressing over salad; taste and adjust seasoning. Cover and refrigerate for at least 2 hours to allow flavors to blend.

Makes 4 to 6 servings.

Couscous and Chick-pea Salad

This is a great salad for summer barbecues, or to take along for a pot-luck. Feel free to add your own variations, by changing the beans or by adding other raw or cooked vegetables, such as shredded carrot, diced green pepper, cooked zucchini or roasted sweet peppers, or dried fruit, such as chopped apricots, cranberries or sour cherries.

Dressing

1/2 cup	olive oil 125 mL
1/2 cup	lemon juice 125 mL
1 tsp	minced garlic 5 mL
1/2 tsp	ground cumin 2 mL
2 to 4 drops	hot pepper sauce 2 to 4 drops
	Salt and pepper, to taste

Salad

3 cups	chicken or vegetable stock 750 mL
2 tbsp	butter, optional 30 mL
2 cups	couscous 500 mL
1	can (19 oz/540 mL) chick-peas, drained and rinsed 1
2/3 cup	currants, plumped in hot water and drained 150 mL
2/3 cup	diced sweet red or yellow pepper 150 mL
1/2 cup	sliced green onions (about 4) 125 mL
1/2 cup	chopped parsley 125 mL
1/4 cup	chopped fresh mint 60 mL
1/3 cup	toasted pine nuts 75 mL

Dressing

1. Whisk together all ingredients; set aside.

Salad

1. In a medium saucepan over high heat, bring stock and butter (if using) to boil. Remove from heat; stir in couscous. Cover and let stand for 10 minutes. Fluff with fork.
2. In a large bowl, mix together couscous and remaining ingredients, except pine nuts. Stir in dressing until well mixed. Cover and let stand at room temperature for about 1 hour. (May be refrigerated overnight; bring to room temperature before serving.) Just before serving, stir in pine nuts.

Makes about 12 side-dish servings.

Variation

Use 2 cups (500 mL) chopped poached or grilled chicken in place of chick-peas; omit currants and stir in 1-1/2 cups (375 mL) diced mango. If desired, use 1/2 cup (125 mL) chopped fresh basil or cilantro in place of mint.

Greek Salad

The Greek Islands are known for oregano, and its taste comes through in this popular salad. Traditional recipes do not include lettuce; replace lettuce with additional cucumber and tomatoes if desired. Add 1 tsp (5 mL) dried oregano to the dressing if you cannot get fresh.

4 cups	torn iceberg lettuce or mesclun mix 1 L
4	large, ripe tomatoes, cut into wedges 4 (or 3/4 lb/375 g cherry tomatoes, halved)
1	medium English cucumber (unpeeled), thinly sliced or chopped 1
1	large sweet red or yellow pepper, chopped into large chunks 1
1/2 cup	thinly sliced sweet onion 125 mL

2 tbsp	chopped fresh oregano 30 mL
2 tbsp	chopped fresh mint leaves, optional 30 mL
1 tbsp	chopped fresh parsley, optional 15 mL
16	Kalamata olives 16
2 tbsp	red wine vinegar 30 mL
1/2 tsp	lemon juice 2 mL
6 tbsp	olive oil 90 mL
	Salt and pepper, to taste
4 oz	feta cheese, crumbled or broken into small pieces 125 g

Note

• Oregano, which translates as "joy of the mountain," has become popular in North America only since the 1940s.
• Kalamata olives are Greek olives, and are deep brown to black in color with an almond-like shape. Look for them in Greek or Italian markets or in bulk in the produce section of major supermarkets.

1. In a large salad bowl, combine lettuce, tomatoes, cucumber, red pepper, onion, oregano, mint and parsley (if using) and olives. Cover and refrigerate until serving.
2. In a small glass measuring cup, whisk together vinegar and lemon juice. Slowly whisk in olive oil. Set aside.
3. When ready to serve, whisk dressing and pour desired amount over salad; toss to coat well. Season with salt and pepper. Top with feta cheese.

Makes 4 servings.

Green Goddess Dressing

Serve this on a salad of greens, topped with avocado slices, shrimp and/or hard-boiled eggs.

1/2 cup	each: loosely packed fresh tarragon and parsley 125 mL
1/2 cup	snipped fresh chives or garlic chives 125 mL
1	small clove garlic, optional 1
1/2 cup	each: sour cream and mayonnaise 125 mL
4 tbsp	olive oil 60 mL
2 tbsp	lemon juice 30 mL
2 tsp	anchovy paste 10 mL
	Salt and pepper, to taste

1. In food processor, blend tarragon, parsley, chives and garlic (if using). Add sour cream, mayonnaise, oil, lemon juice, anchovy paste and a little salt and pepper; purée just until smooth. Chill for several hours to thicken.
2. Taste and adjust seasoning. Use within 3 days.

Makes about 1-2/3 cups (400 mL).

Herb Salad

Basil, tarragon and chervil all have anise or licorice undertones, making them perfect salad companions. They are used here with the perfect backdrop of mild-tasting lettuces. Make use of herb flowers or other edible flowers for the finishing touch.

Salad

1	head red leaf lettuce	1
1	head Boston lettuce	1
2 cups	coarsely chopped fresh basil or purple basil	500 mL
1 cup	coarsely chopped fresh tarragon	250 mL
1 cup	coarsely chopped fresh chervil	250 mL
1 cup	chopped fresh chives	250 mL
	Vinaigrette (recipe follows)	
	Herb flowers and other edible flowers (see "Edible Flowers," page 38), for garnish	

1. Tear lettuce leaves into bite-sized pieces; toss with herbs in large bowl; refrigerate.
2. Just before serving toss with a little Vinaigrette to taste; garnish with herb flowers and other edible flowers.

Vinaigrette

1/4 cup	white wine or herb vinegar (such as chive blossom, purple basil or tarragon)	60 mL
1 tsp	Dijon mustard or Herb Mustard (see page 27)	5 mL
1/2 tsp	granulated sugar	2 mL
1/4 tsp	salt	1 mL
	Pepper, to taste	
1 cup	sunflower oil	250 mL

1. In a small bowl, whisk together vinegar, mustard, sugar, salt and pepper.
2. Slowly whisk in oil. Store in refrigerator up to 4 weeks.

Makes 6 servings.

Note

All flowers of culinary herbs are edible. The flavor will be similar to the herb it comes from. In some cases, such as with chive flowers, the taste will be quite strong, so separate chive flowers into florets if desired.

Herbed Asparagus Salad

This salad is a perfect side dish for grilled fish or chicken—crispy, barely cooked fresh asparagus spears in a tangy herb vinaigrette.

Salad

1 lb	asparagus, cut into 1-1/2-inch/4 cm pieces 500 g
3/4 cup	sliced water chestnuts 175 mL
1/4 cup	diced red onion (or cut into slivers) 60 mL

Dressing

2 tbsp	each: oil and white wine vinegar 30 mL
1 tbsp	finely chopped fresh dill or tarragon 15 mL
1 tsp	Dijon mustard 5 mL
1/4 tsp	granulated sugar 1 mL
1	small clove garlic, crushed 1
	Salt and pepper, to taste

Salad

1. Put asparagus in a medium saucepan of boiling water; return to boil and cook for 3 to 4 minutes or just until tender. Drain asparagus; chill in cold water. Drain again; dry on paper towel.
2. In a medium bowl, mix together asparagus, water chestnuts and onion.

Dressing

1. Whisk together all ingredients.
2. Pour over salad; toss to coat well. Salad may be made up to 4 hours ahead and refrigerated.

Makes 4 servings.

Marinated Vegetable and Chick-pea Salad

This is a great make-ahead salad that is full of crunchy vegetables. The chick-peas add a boost of fiber. Serve with roasted or grilled chicken, pork kebabs or sausage.

Salad

3 cups	cauliflower, cut into bite-size pieces 750 mL
2 cups	thinly sliced carrots 500 mL
2	small zucchini, sliced 2
1	red pepper, cut into bite-size pieces 1
1	green pepper, cut into bite-size pieces 1
1	can (19 oz/540 mL) chick-peas, drained and rinsed 1

Marinade

1/2 cup	olive oil 125 mL
1/4 cup	red wine vinegar 60 mL
2	cloves garlic, minced 2
2 tbsp	each: finely chopped fresh basil and parsley 30 mL
1 tbsp	finely chopped fresh oregano, marjoram or savory 15 mL (or 1 tsp/5 mL dried)
1 tsp	granulated sugar 5 mL
	Salt and pepper, to taste

1. In a large saucepan of boiling water, cook cauliflower and carrots until tender crisp, about 2 minutes. Drain and plunge into cold water; drain well and place in large bowl. Add zucchini, peppers and chick-peas.
2. Whisk together marinade ingredients, pour over vegetables and toss. Cover tightly with plastic wrap or transfer to large zip-lock bag. Refrigerate for at least 4 hours or up to 2 days. Stir mixture or turn bag occasionally.

Makes about 10 cups (2.5 L).

Orzo Salad

Orzo is a tiny rice-shaped pasta that works well in this Greek-style salad. Serve with lamb, pork or chicken kebabs.

1-1/2 cups	orzo	375 mL
1/3 cup	chopped, soft sun-dried tomatoes	75 mL
12	cherry tomatoes, quartered	12
1/2 cup	each: diced sweet red and yellow pepper	125 mL
1/2 cup	crumbled feta	125 mL
1/3 cup	diced red or Vidalia onion	75 mL
1/4 cup	each: finely chopped fresh basil and parsley	60 mL
1 tbsp	finely chopped fresh oregano (or 1 tsp/5 mL dried)	15 mL
1/4 cup	red wine vinegar	60 mL
2 tbsp	olive oil	30 mL
12 to 15	Kalamata olives	12 to 15

1. In a large saucepan of boiling, salted water, cook orzo just until tender; drain. Rinse with cold water and drain well.
2. In a large bowl, mix together orzo, sun-dried and cherry tomatoes, peppers, feta, onion, basil, parsley and oregano.
3. Whisk together vinegar and oil; pour over salad and toss. Garnish with olives.

Makes 6 servings.

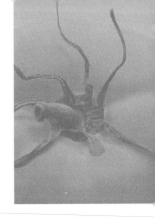

Panzanella

This is the great bread salad from Tuscany, Italy. It's a must to make at the peak of tomato season. If desired, add any of the following: artichoke hearts, asparagus, cannellini (white kidney) beans, cubed mozzarella, finely chopped capers.

1/3 cup	olive oil 75 mL
2 tbsp	each: red wine vinegar and lemon juice 30 mL
	Salt and pepper, to taste
1/4 cup	minced fresh parsley 60 mL
3 cups	torn day-old Italian bread 750 mL
3	large ripe tomatoes, chopped 3
2 cups	peeled, seeded and chopped cucumbers 500 mL
1 cup	chopped or sliced red onion 250 mL
1	large clove garlic, crushed 1
1/2 cup	sliced fresh basil 125 mL
1/3 cup	Kalamata olives 75 mL

1. In a small bowl, whisk together oil, vinegar, lemon juice and a little salt and pepper. Stir in parsley; reserve.
2. In a large bowl, mix together bread, tomatoes, cucumbers, onion, garlic, basil and olives. Add reserved dressing and toss well. Taste and season with more salt and pepper if desired. Serve immediately.

Makes about 4 servings.

Variations

Bread Salad from Crete: Add 2 tbsp (30 mL) each: chopped fresh oregano and mint, and 3/4 cup (175 mL) cubed feta cheese.

Fattoush (Lebanese): Omit red wine vinegar and use 3 tbsp (45 mL) lemon juice altogether. Use torn pita bread in place of Italian bread. Use 2 tbsp (30 mL) chopped mint or cilantro in place of basil; omit olives. Add 1 cup (250 mL) cooked, drained chick-peas, optional.

Parsleyed Croutons

So much better than store-bought! Crunchy on the outside and soft on the inside. Use for salads or to garnish creamed soups.

2 tbsp	butter 30 mL
2 cups	cubed stale bread (French, Italian, pumpernickel, etc.), crusts removed, cut into 3/4-inch (6 mm) cubes 500 mL
3 tbsp	finely chopped fresh parsley 45 mL
	Seasoning salt

1. In a large skillet over medium heat, melt butter. Stir in bread cubes; toss to coat well.
2. Stir in parsley; sprinkle with seasoning salt. Cook, stirring often, until lightly browned and crisp. Let cool. Store for up to 5 days in glass jar.

Makes 2 cups (500 mL).

Variation

Use 1 tbsp (15 mL) finely chopped sage or lemon thyme in place of 1 tbsp (15 mL) of the parsley.

Potato Salad with Dill-Chive Vinaigrette

Contrive your own delicious version to enjoy for summer barbecues and picnics. Add any of the following: sliced avocado, chopped sun-dried tomatoes, wedges of hard-cooked eggs, cooked peas, sweet red or yellow peppers (roasted, if desired), sliced celery or radishes, crisply cooked asparagus tips.

Salad

3 lb	medium or small red-skinned potatoes 1.5 kg
1/3 cup	diced white or red onion (or sliced green onions) 75 mL
1/4 cup	chopped fresh parsley 60 mL
1/2 to 3/4 cup	Dill-Chive Vinaigrette (recipe follows) 125 to 175 mL
	Salt and pepper, to taste

1. Halve or quarter potatoes. In a large saucepan of boiling salted water, cook potatoes for 8 to 10 minutes or until tender. Drain; let cool.
2. In a large bowl, mix together potatoes, onion and parsley. Gently stir in enough dressing to coat potatoes. Add salt and pepper to taste.

Makes 8 servings.

> **tip**
>
> To prepare dressing in food processor, combine all ingredients except oil; pulse to mix. With machine running slowly, drizzle in oil; process until well combined and slightly thickened.

Dill-Chive Vinaigrette

This is a very versatile dressing. Pour it over tender-crisp cooked green beans, peas or cauliflower. Serve over a salad of asparagus, new potatoes, hard-cooked eggs and tomato wedges.

1 tbsp	white wine vinegar 15 mL
1 tbsp	lemon juice 15 mL
1 tbsp	Dijon mustard 15 mL
1/2 tsp	granulated sugar 2 mL
1 cup	oil 250 mL
1/3 cup	chopped fresh dill 75 mL
1/4 cup	chopped fresh chives 60 mL
	Salt and pepper, to taste

1. In a small bowl, whisk together vinegar, lemon juice, mustard and sugar.
2. Gradually whisk in oil. Stir in dill and chives. Season with salt and pepper. Refrigerate for up to 1 week. Shake or stir before using.

Makes 1-1/4 cups (300 mL).

Roasted Beet Salad with Dill-Chive Vinaigrette

This is a scrumptious and colorful little salad that is sure to impress. The beets have a wonderful sweet taste that is accented by the orange and mint. It's my favorite way to eat beets.

3 to 4	medium beets 3 to 4
1	head Boston or red leaf lettuce 1
2	large oranges, peeled and sliced 2
4 tbsp	toasted walnut pieces, optional 60 mL
	Dill-Chive Vinaigrette (see page 96)
	Dill sprigs, for garnish

1. Cut tops off beets, leaving about 1 inch (2.5 cm) of stem. Wrap individually in foil. Place on baking sheet; roast in a 375°F (190°C) oven for about 1-1/2 hours, or until tender when pierced with knife. Let cool; slip off skins. (This may be done ahead; wrap beets in plastic wrap and refrigerate.)

2. Cut beets into slices about 1/4 inch (5 mm) thick. Arrange lettuce on 4 individual serving plates; alternate beet slices with orange slices.

3. Just before serving, top each serving with 1 tbsp (15 mL) walnuts (if using); drizzle with Dill-Chive Vinaigrette. Garnish with dill sprigs.

Makes 4 servings.

Note

Beets are rich in anthocyanins, which are powerful antioxidants and play a role in prevention of heart disease.

Spinach Salad with Creamy Herb Yogurt Dressing

This tasty salad can be served as a starter, or for the main course with a nice loaf of grainy bread.

Salad

8 cups	torn spinach leaves	2 L
1 cup	thinly sliced button mushrooms	250 mL
3	hard-cooked eggs, chopped	3
1/3 cup	bacon bits	75 mL
	Creamy Herb Yogurt Dressing (recipe follows)	

1. Divide spinach among 4 individual plates. Top each with 1/4 cup (60 mL) of the sliced mushrooms.
2. Sprinkle eggs over each salad; top with bacon bits.
3. Chill until ready to serve. Drizzle with Creamy Herb Yogurt Dressing.

Variation

For creamy Herb Yogurt Dressing: Use 1 tbsp (15 mL) chopped fresh dill in place of the basil and tarragon.

Creamy Herb Yogurt Dressing

For a super low-fat dressing, use no-fat yogurt and low-fat mayonnaise.

1 cup	plain yogurt	250 mL
1/2 cup	mayonnaise	125 mL
2 tsp	lemon juice	10 mL
1	clove garlic, crushed	1
1/4 tsp	paprika	1 mL
1 tbsp	each: chopped fresh basil and tarragon	15 mL
1 tbsp	chopped fresh chives, optional	15 mL
	Salt and pepper, to taste	

1. In a small bowl, whisk together yogurt, mayonnaise, lemon juice, garlic and paprika until smooth.
2. Stir in basil, tarragon and chives (if using). Season with salt and pepper.
3. Chill dressing until ready to serve. Keeps for 1 to 2 days in the refrigerator.

Makes 4 servings.

Spinach Salad with Grilled Asparagus, Parmesan and Mint

This salad (recipe contributed by Foodland Ontario) would make a wonderful light lunch or supper when served with fresh bread.

12 oz	asparagus, trimmed 375 g
	Olive oil for brushing
	Salt and pepper, to taste
1/4 cup	olive oil 60 mL
1/4 cup	finely chopped fresh mint 60 mL
2 tbsp	lemon juice 30 mL
1 tbsp	honey mustard 15 mL
1	clove garlic, minced 1
8 cups	fresh spinach, trimmed and torn into bite-size pieces 2L
1/2 cup	thinly slivered red onion 125 mL
2	slices prosciutto, chopped (or cooked and crumbled bacon) 2
1/4 cup	shaved Parmesan cheese 60 mL (or 2 tbsp/30 mL grated)

1. Line up asparagus spears in a row; skewer through center using metal or soaked bamboo skewers. Lightly brush with oil; sprinkle with salt and pepper.
2. Barbecue over medium heat for 3 to 6 minutes or until tender. Cut into 2-inch (5 cm) pieces.
3. In a small bowl, whisk together 1/4 cup (60 mL) oil, mint, lemon juice, mustard, garlic and a little salt and pepper.
4. In a large bowl, place asparagus, spinach, onion and prosciutto. Toss with just enough dressing to coat. Divide among 4 to 6 individual serving plates. Top each serving with a little Parmesan cheese.

Makes 4 to 6 servings.

Tabbouleh Salad

Middle Eastern in origin, this crunchy grain salad is a natural for fresh herbs. It has a minty cool, fresh taste perfect for summertime meals. Serve with barbecued chicken or lamb.

1 cup	bulgur	250 mL
2 cups	boiling water	500 mL
1 cup	seeded, diced English cucumber	250 mL
14	cherry tomatoes, quartered	14
1/2 cup	finely chopped fresh parsley	125 mL
1/4 cup	snipped fresh chives	60 mL
2 tbsp	finely chopped fresh mint	30 mL
4 tbsp	olive oil	60 mL
2 tbsp	lemon juice	30 mL
1	small clove garlic, minced	1
	Salt and pepper, to taste	

1. In a large bowl, place bulgur; stir in boiling water. Cover and let stand for 30 minutes. Drain well, using spoon to press out excess water; let cool to room temperature.
2. Mix together bulgur, cucumber, tomatoes, parsley, chives and mint.
3. In a small bowl, whisk together oil, lemon juice and garlic; pour over salad and mix well. Season with salt and pepper. Refrigerate for at least an hour or for up to 6 hours. Remove from refrigerator 15 minutes before serving.

Makes 6 servings.

Tangy Thai Coleslaw

This low-fat, vitamin-packed coleslaw is a favorite of Dana McCauley, food editor of *Homemaker's* magazine (where it has appeared) and cookbook author. She recommends serving it with grilled lean flank steak. I also think it would be great with grilled chicken breast or oven-roasted chicken.

Dressing

2 tbsp	orange juice 30 mL
1 tbsp	light soy sauce or tamari 15 mL
1 tbsp	rice wine vinegar 15 mL
1 tsp	minced fresh ginger 5 mL
1/2 tsp	each: granulated sugar and grated orange rind 2 mL
dash	hot pepper sauce dash
2 tsp	sesame oil 10 mL

Salad

2 cups	finely shredded napa or Savoy cabbage 500 mL
1/2 cup	each: coarsely shredded carrots, thinly sliced snow peas and finely diced mango 125 mL
1/4 cup	each: thinly sliced red onion, bean sprouts 60 mL
2 tbsp	chopped fresh cilantro 30 mL

1. In a small bowl, whisk together orange juice, soy sauce, vinegar, fresh ginger, sugar, orange rind and hot pepper sauce. Whisking constantly, drizzle in sesame oil until well combined. Reserve.

2. In a large bowl, mix together cabbage, carrots, snow peas, mango, onion, bean sprouts and cilantro. Add dressing; toss until well combined. Taste and adjust seasoning if necessary.

Makes 4 servings.

Tarragon and Caper Mayonnaise

Serve with cold potatoes, asparagus, shrimp, hard-cooked eggs, crab and/or lobster.

2	egg yolks	2
3 tbsp	white wine vinegar	45 mL
1 tbsp	each: finely chopped chives, tarragon and parsley	15 mL
1 tbsp	Dijon mustard	15 mL
2 tsp	capers	10 mL
1	small clove garlic, crushed	1
	Salt and pepper, to taste	
1 cup	oil	250 mL

1. In food processor, combine egg yolks, vinegar, chives, tarragon, parsley, mustard, capers and garlic. Add a little salt and pepper; process until smooth.
2. With food processor running, slowly drizzle in oil. Refrigerate for up to 5 days.

Makes about 1-1/4 cups (300 mL).

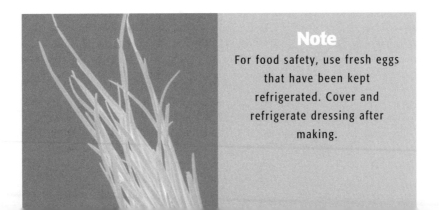

Note

For food safety, use fresh eggs that have been kept refrigerated. Cover and refrigerate dressing after making.

Tomato Salad with Basil Cream Dressing

I always make this salad mid-summer when my cherry tomato "trees" are overflowing with these little, red, so-sweet jewels. You can also make a salad of garden leaf lettuce, topped with regular tomato wedges, sliced onions or snipped chives and basil, and drizzled with a dressing of sour cream and vinegar.

3 cups	halved cherry tomatoes or grape tomatoes 750 mL
1/4 cup	diced or thinly sliced red onion or green onions 60 mL
1/4 cup	chiffonade of fresh basil (see page x) 60 mL
1/4 cup	sour cream 60 mL
1 to 2 tbsp	red wine vinegar or balsamic vinegar 15 to 30 mL

1. In a medium bowl, combine tomatoes, onion and basil.
2. In a small bowl, whisk together sour cream and vinegar; pour over salad and stir to combine well. Cover and let stand for an hour to allow flavors to develop.

Makes 4 servings.

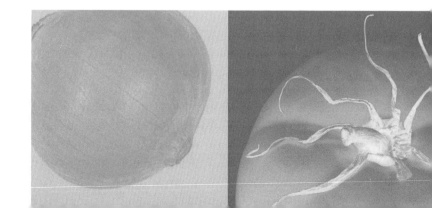

Tomatoes and Bocconcini with Basil

This recipe is a favorite of Carol Ferguson, and appears in her *The New Canadian Basics Cookbook* (Penguin Books Canada Ltd., 1999). This makes a beautiful salad platter for a hot summer day when garden tomatoes and fresh basil are at their peak. Serve with crusty Italian bread. Be sure to use top-quality cheese and olive oil.

4	ripe tomatoes, sliced	4
1/2 lb	sliced bocconcini cheese	250 g
	Salt and pepper, to taste	
1/2 cup	chiffonade of fresh basil (see page x)	125 mL
1/4 cup	snipped fresh chives (or 2 tbsp/30 mL chopped Italian parsley)	60 mL
6 tbsp	extra-virgin olive oil	90 mL
2 tbsp	balsamic or red wine vinegar	30 mL

1. On a large platter or 4 individual salad plates, alternate tomato and cheese slices, overlapping slightly.
2. Sprinkle lightly with salt and a few grindings of fresh pepper. Sprinkle with basil and chives.
3. Drizzle with oil and vinegar.

Makes 4 servings.

Variation

Tomatoes and Feta: Use crumbled feta cheese instead of bocconcini; sprinkle over tomato slices. Instead of basil and chives, sprinkle with 2 tbsp (30 mL) each finely chopped basil and oregano (or marjoram), and 1 tsp (5 mL) finely chopped fresh thyme or lemon thyme. This is excellent served as a side dish for grilled chicken.

Note

Bocconcini are small balls of a mild Italian cheese similar to mozzarella; the term translates as "small mouthfuls."

Herbs give a flavor infusion to marinades for meats, add a splash of excitement to fish and seafood and naturally go with eggs. Use herbal oils, vinegars and mustards in marinades. Fresh herbs in mustards, sauces and salsas accent meat and seafood dishes. Douse eggs with almost any fresh herb. Place a dab of herb butter over meats, fish or seafood just before serving—the warmth of the food melts the butter and releases the flavor. Chopped fresh parsley can be added to any dish to add lively color.

MEAT, SEAFOOD AND EGGS

Recipes

Focaccia Sandwiches

These sandwiches "stack up" great taste! The tarragon in the mayonnaise complements the beef very well.

1	large loaf focaccia bread	1
1/2 cup	Tarragon and Caper Mayonnaise (see page 102)	125 mL
1 lb	sliced roast beef, turkey or chicken	500 g
1	bunch arugula	1
2	large roasted yellow peppers, sliced	2
2	large tomatoes, thinly sliced	2
1	small red onion, thinly sliced	1

1. Slice bread in half horizontally. Spread bottom half generously with Tarragon and Caper Mayonnaise.
2. Layer meat on top of the mayonnaise; add arugula, peppers, tomatoes and onion.
3. Replace top of bread. Secure with toothpicks; cut into wedges or rectangles.

Makes 4 servings.

Variations
- Use grilled eggplant slices in place of the meat.
- Use pesto in place of Tarragon and Caper Mayonnaise, and roasted or grilled chicken in place of beef.

Note
If you don't have time to make the Tarragon and Caper Mayonnaise, stir 1 tbsp (15 mL) finely chopped fresh tarragon into 1/2 cup (125 mL) store-bought mayonnaise.

Grilled Steak with Bernaise Sauce

Meats don't always have to be marinated to get the taste of herbs. Bernaise is a classic herb sauce to serve with steak, and is not that hard to make. Also very good is Tarragon-Dijon Butter (see page 32) placed on top of a steak just before serving. The Bernaise Sauce is also delicious over asparagus.

4	filet mignon or boneless sirloin steaks, 6 to 8 oz (175 to 250 g) each; or New York steaks, about 1 inch (2.5 cm) thick 4
1	clove garlic, optional 1
	Freshly ground pepper

1. Let steaks rest, covered, at room temperature, for 30 minutes. Cut garlic in half lengthwise (if using); rub over surface of steaks. Season with a few grinds of pepper (do not add salt).

2. Place on heated barbecue grill or grill pan on top of stove over medium-high heat. Grill, turning only once. For rare, cook for 5 to 7 minutes total; for medium-rare, 7 to 9 minutes; for medium, 9 to 11 minutes; for medium-well, 11 to 13 minutes; for well, 13 to 15 minutes. Serve with Bernaise Sauce in a side dish.

Makes 4 servings.

Note

• Salt tends to draw the water out of the meat, toughening it; add salt after cooking if desired.
• If you do not have a double boiler, use a heat-proof bowl placed on top of a saucepan.

Bernaise Sauce

1/4 cup	white wine vinegar (or tarragon vinegar)	60 mL
2 tsp	finely chopped fresh tarragon	10 mL
2 tsp	finely chopped fresh chervil, optional	10 mL
1 tbsp	finely chopped shallots	15 mL
3	peppercorns, crushed	3
pinch	salt	pinch
4	egg yolks	4
1/2 cup	butter, softened	125 mL

1. In a small saucepan over high heat, mix together vinegar, 1 tsp (5 mL) each of the tarragon and chervil (if using), shallots, pepper and salt. Bring to a boil; reduce heat and simmer, uncovered, for about 5 minutes, until liquid is reduced by half. Strain; discard solids.

2. In the top of a double boiler (off heat), place egg yolks. Whisk in herbed vinegar mixture well.

3. Place double boiler over boiling water. Gradually whisk in butter a little at a time; whisk until sauce thickens.

4. Remove from heat; stir in remaining 1 tsp (5 mL) each of the tarragon and chervil (if using). Keep warm until ready to use.

Makes about 1 cup (250 mL).

Osso Bucco with Gremolata

This classic Italian dish is made from veal shanks simmered in a herb, wine and tomato sauce until tender. The marrow found inside the bone is considered a delicacy. Serve with mashed potatoes or rice.

3 tbsp	olive oil	45 mL
2 cups	diced carrots (4 or 5 carrots)	500 mL
1-1/2 cups	diced onion	375 mL
2	stalks celery, diced	2
3	large cloves garlic, minced	3
3 tbsp	chopped fresh thyme	45 mL
3	bay leaves	3
6	veal shanks (about 3 lb/1.5 kg)	6
	Salt and pepper, to taste	
1/4 cup	all-purpose flour	60 mL
1 cup	dry white wine	250 mL
1 cup (approx.)	beef stock	250 mL
1	can (28 oz/796 mL) diced tomatoes	1

1. In a large skillet over medium heat, heat 1 tbsp (15 mL) of the oil. Add carrots, onion and celery; cook for about 7 minutes, until carrots are almost soft. Add garlic, thyme and bay leaves; cook for 2 minutes. Transfer to large oven-proof casserole.

2. Add remaining 2 tbsp (30 mL) of the oil to skillet and increase heat to medium-high. Season veal with salt and pepper, coat with flour. Cook veal for about 4 minutes on each side or until browned. Transfer to baking dish containing vegetables.

3. Add wine and stock to skillet; bring to a boil, stirring to loosen browned bits. Pour over veal; stir in tomatoes, including juice. If necessary, add more broth to almost cover veal.

4. Cover and bake in a 375°F (190°C) oven for about 1-1/2 hours, or until meat is very tender and starting to separate from bones. Before serving, remove bay leaves. If necessary, boil sauce on stovetop to reduce slightly. Place veal on plate, spoon sauce over top and sprinkle with Gremolata (recipe follows).

Makes 4 to 6 servings.

Gremolata

1/2 cup	chopped fresh parsley	125 mL
1 tbsp	grated lemon rind	15 mL
2	cloves garlic, minced	2

1. In a small bowl, mix together all ingredients.

Note

After sautéeing 1/2-inch (1 cm) slices of yellow summer squash or zucchini in a little olive oil until tender, toss in a little Gremolata to taste.

Saltimbocca

Saltimbocca, which means "jumps in the mouth" in Italian, is traditionally made with veal, but is equally delicious with chicken. Just use boneless, skinless chicken breasts and flatten them with a mallet; use dry white wine instead of Marsala.

1 lb	thinly sliced veal scallopini (8 pieces) 500 g
8	slices prosciutto 8
16	whole fresh sage leaves 16
4 oz	Parmesan cheese, thinly sliced 125 g
1 tbsp	each: butter and olive oil 15 mL
3/4 cup	Marsala wine 175 mL
1 tbsp	lemon juice 15 mL
1 to 2 tbsp	chopped fresh parsley 15 to 30 mL

1. Top each veal slice with a slice of prosciutto; place 2 large sage leaves on top. Top with a slice of Parmesan.
2. Roll up each assembled piece, securing with a strong toothpick.
3. In a large skillet over medium heat, heat butter and oil. Add veal rolls; cook for 6 to 8 minutes until well browned on all sides. Remove from pan; keep warm.
4. Add wine to pan; stir with wooden spoon to scrape browned bits from the bottom of the pan. Stir in lemon juice; simmer until reduced and thickened (almost syrupy).
5. Place 2 veal rolls on each individual plate; drizzle with sauce and sprinkle with parsley.

Makes 4 servings.

Cherry Chicken with Rosemary and Orange

Cherries partner well with poultry. This recipe is a delicious combination of savory and sweet. Serve with mashed potatoes or a mixture of white and wild rice.

1 lb	boneless skinless chicken breast 500 g
	Salt and pepper, to taste
2 tbsp	all-purpose flour 30 mL
2 tbsp	butter 30 mL
1/2 cup	finely chopped shallots 125 mL
1 tbsp	minced fresh rosemary 15 mL
3/4 cup	dry white wine 175 mL
1/3 cup	orange marmalade 75 mL
2 tsp	Dijon mustard 10 mL
2 cups	sweet cherries, pitted and halved 500 mL
	Rosemary sprigs, for garnish

1. Flatten or cut chicken to 1/2-inch (1 cm) thickness; season with salt and pepper and dredge in flour. In a large skillet over medium heat, heat 1 tbsp (15 mL) of the butter. Cook chicken until golden, for about 3 minutes on each side; remove from pan.
2. Put remaining 1 tbsp (15 mL) of the butter in the pan. Add shallots and rosemary; cook for 3 minutes or until softened. Stir in wine, marmalade and mustard.
3. Return chicken to pan; add cherries. Reduce heat; simmer for about 10 minutes or until sauce is thickened. Serve with cherry sauce spooned over chicken. Garnish with rosemary sprigs.

Makes 4 servings.

Chicken Breasts Provençal

The Provence region of southern France is known for its use of garlic, tomatoes and olives or olive oil in its cooking. A dash of wine and handful of herbs and you'll almost feel like you are there! I have tried this dish with a little crumbled feta cheese added to it just before serving and it was terrific.

3 tbsp	olive oil 45 mL
4	boneless, skinless chicken breasts 4 (or 8 skinless thighs)
1/4 cup	all-purpose flour 60 mL
	Salt and pepper, to taste
1/2 cup	diced onions or shallots 125 mL
2	cloves garlic, minced 2
1/2 cup	white wine 125 mL
3 cups	chopped tomatoes (3 or 4 large) 750 mL (or 28 oz/796 mL can diced tomatoes, drained)
16	black olives, halved and pitted 16
1 tbsp	packed brown sugar, optional 15 mL
1 tbsp	chopped fresh marjoram or oregano 15 mL
2 tsp	each: finely chopped fresh rosemary and tarragon 10 mL

1. In a large skillet over medium-high, heat 2 tbsp (30 mL) of the oil. Dredge chicken in flour; sprinkle with salt and pepper. Cook for 2 to 3 minutes per side to brown; remove from pan.
2. Reduce heat to medium-low; add remaining 1 tbsp (15 mL) of the oil to pan. Stir in onions and garlic; cook for 3 to 5 minutes or until softened.
3. Stir in wine, scraping up browned bits from the bottom of the pan. Stir in tomatoes, olives and brown sugar (if using).
4. Return chicken and juices to pan. Cover; simmer for 15 minutes.
5. Remove lid. Increase heat to medium; cook uncovered for 10 to 12 minutes to thicken sauce.
6. Stir in marjoram, rosemary and tarragon; cook for 3 minutes.

Makes 4 servings.

Variation

Use shrimp instead of chicken but cook sauce alone, uncovered, over medium heat for about 8 to 10 minutes to thicken. Then add peeled, deveined shrimp and cook for 2 to 3 minutes, until shrimp is just cooked through (do not overcook). Serve with rice.

Chicken Piccata

Tender chicken in a light lemon sauce (more of a glaze) with a hint of tarragon is quick to prepare. Serve with steamed broccoli or green beans and rice.

4	boneless, skinless chicken breasts 4
	Salt and pepper, to taste
1/4 cup	all-purpose flour 60 mL
1 tbsp	each: butter and oil 15 mL
1/3 cup	dry white wine 75 mL
1 tbsp	chopped fresh tarragon 15 mL
1 tbsp	lemon juice 15 mL
	Lemon slices and tarragon sprigs, for garnish

1. Flatten chicken breasts using a meat mallet. Season with a little salt and pepper. Dredge chicken in flour, shaking off excess.
2. In a large non-stick skillet over medium heat, heat butter and oil. Add chicken; cook for about 3 minutes per side or until lightly browned.
3. Add wine and tarragon to pan, turning chicken to coat. Cover; cook for 2 to 3 minutes. Sprinkle with lemon juice. Garnish plate with lemon slices and small tarragon sprigs.

Makes 4 servings.

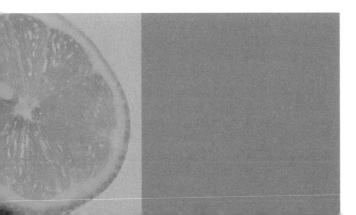

Chicken Tikka Masala

This is a delicious East Indian dish full of exotic spices and accented with fresh herbs—cilantro and mint. Go easy on the hot chilis if you like it mild. Serve with Raita (see page 142) for a touch of coolness. Add cooked basmati rice and warmed naan bread to complete the meal.

1 cup	chopped onions 250 mL
2	cloves garlic, crushed 2
1/4 cup	tomato paste 60 mL
1/4 cup	lemon juice 60 mL
1 tbsp	grated fresh ginger 15 mL
1 tsp	each: ground coriander, cumin and chili powder 5 mL
	Salt and pepper, to taste
1-1/2 lb	boneless skinless chicken breast 750 g
2 tbsp	oil 30 mL
1	large onion, halved and sliced 1
2	cloves garlic, crushed 2
1	chopped green chili pepper, or to taste 1
1 cup	drained diced tomatoes (fresh or canned) 250 mL
1/2 cup	each: plain yogurt and coconut milk 125 mL
1 tbsp	each: finely chopped fresh cilantro and mint 15 mL
	Mint sprigs, for garnish

1. In food processor, place chopped onions, 2 cloves garlic, tomato paste, lemon juice, ginger, coriander, cumin and chili powder. Add a little salt and pepper. Process until smooth.
2. Cut chicken into 1-1/2-inch (4 cm) cubes. In a large bowl, mix together chicken and marinade. Cover and refrigerate for at least 2 hours or overnight.
3. In a large skillet over medium heat, heat oil. Add sliced onion; cook for about 7 minutes or until softened. Stir in garlic and chili pepper; cook for 1 minute.
4. Drain excess marinade from chicken; add chicken to skillet. Cook, stirring, for 5 minutes or until chicken is cooked through.
5. Stir in tomatoes, yogurt and coconut milk. Reduce heat; cover and simmer for about 20 minutes.
6. Remove from heat; stir in cilantro and mint. Garnish with mint sprigs.

Makes 4 servings.

Cranberry Orange and Rosemary Stuffed Chicken or Turkey Breast

Chicken breasts are stuffed with an orange and herb cream cheese filling, coated in savory crumbs and baked.

1	pkg (8 oz/250 g) cream cheese, softened	1
1/4 cup	chopped dried cranberries	60 mL
4 tsp	orange juice concentrate	20 mL
1 tbsp	finely chopped fresh chives	15 mL
1 tbsp	chopped fresh parsley	15 mL
1 tsp	grated orange rind	5 mL
1	clove garlic, finely chopped	1
6	boneless, skinless chicken or turkey breasts (6 oz/175 g each)	6

Crumb Coating

2 cups	fresh breadcrumbs	500 mL
1/4 cup	butter, melted	60 mL
1/4 cup	chopped fresh parsley	60 mL
2 tbsp	minced fresh rosemary	30 mL
1 tsp	seasoning salt or salt	5 mL
2	eggs, beaten	2

1. In a medium bowl, mix together cream cheese, cranberries, juice concentrate, chives, 1 tbsp (15 mL) of the parsley and garlic until well combined; chill to firm up slightly.

2. Place chicken between two pieces of waxed paper; pound to flatten, until 1/4 inch (5mm) thick. Divide filling among chicken breasts, placing at one edge; fold in sides and roll up, sealing completely. Wrap rolls tightly with plastic wrap and refrigerate for at least 30 minutes.

3. In a medium bowl combine breadcrumbs, melted butter, parsley, rosemary and seasoning salt. Dip each roll in eggs then in breadcrumb mixture, pressing to coat well. Place on a lightly greased baking sheet. Bake in a 375°F (190°C) oven for 25 to 30 minutes, until golden and tender.

Makes 6 servings.

Note

make ahead and freeze, complete with crumb ating, wrap tightly with plastic wrap; place in eezer bag or container nd freezer. Bake from frozen, adding about 5 minutes to the cooking time.

Variation

Chicken Kiev: Make Fines Herbes Butter (see page 31), omitting chervil and shallots. Divide butter into 6 portions; form into small logs and chill or freeze until firm. Use butter in place of cream cheese filling.

Herb-Roasted Chicken with Roasted Garlic

This is a dish you will want to make over and over. The herb flavors penetrate the meat to give a wonderful taste. Serve with mashed potatoes and roasted squash, green beans, Brussels sprouts or carrots.

1	whole roasting chicken, about 4 lb (2 kg) 1
	Salt and pepper, to taste
4 to 6 sprigs	each: fresh rosemary, sage, savory, thyme or lemon thyme 4 to 6
2	heads garlic, separated into cloves 2
	Olive oil

Note
Herb sprigs should be about 4 inches (10 cm) in length. Sage sprigs will have 4 to 6 leaves on each.

1. Rinse chicken and pat dry with a paper towel. Sprinkle inside of cavity with salt and pepper. Place 2 or 3 sprigs of each herb in cavity.
2. Gently peel skin away from breast of chicken. Reserving 2 sprigs of sage, tuck remaining sprigs of herbs between flesh and skin; pull skin over top.
3. Place chicken on a rack in a roasting pan; surround with garlic cloves and leaves from the reserved 2 sprigs of sage. Brush chicken with olive oil and drizzle some over the garlic. Cover with foil.
4. Roast in a 375°F (190°C) oven for 30 minutes. Remove foil; roast for 45 to 60 minutes longer, basting occasionally, until chicken is golden brown and juices run clear when thigh is pierced with the point of a sharp knife.
5. Slice chicken, discarding the herbs from under the skin. Serve with roasted garlic (squeeze softened garlic from cloves) and sage.

Makes 4 servings.

Lemon and Thyme Chicken with Mushroom Couscous

This is a very quick and satisfying dish to make. If you wish, substitute lemon thyme for the regular thyme and omit lemon rind.

2	boneless chicken breasts, thinly sliced 2
2 tbsp	all-purpose flour 30 mL
2 tbsp	olive oil 30 mL
1-1/2 cups	chicken or vegetable stock 375 mL
1 tbsp	chopped fresh thyme 15 mL
1/2 cup	finely chopped red onion 125 mL
1	clove garlic, minced 1
1/2 lb	brown mushrooms, sliced 250 g
1/2 cup	diced sweet yellow pepper 125 mL
2 tbsp	grated lemon rind 30 mL
1 cup	couscous 250 mL
1/4 cup	finely chopped roasted red peppers 60 mL
	Salt and pepper, to taste

1. Lightly coat chicken with flour. In a very large skillet over medium heat, heat 1 tbsp (15 mL) of the oil. Add chicken; cook, stirring frequently, until lightly browned.

2. Add 1/4 cup (60 mL) of the stock; stir in thyme. Cook until most of the liquid has evaporated. Transfer mixture to a bowl; cover and keep warm.

3. In the same skillet over medium heat, heat remaining 1 tbsp (15 mL) of the oil. Add onion and garlic; cook for 2 minutes. Add mushrooms, yellow pepper and lemon rind; cook for 3 to 5 minutes or until mushrooms are softened.

4. Add remaining 1-1/4 cups (300 mL) of the stock. Increase heat to high; bring to a boil. Stir in couscous and roasted red peppers. Cover; remove from heat. Let rest for 5 minutes.

5. Stir in reserved chicken; season with salt and pepper.

Makes 4 servings.

Note

Couscous has been gaining in popularity for its versatility and very quick cooking time. It is not a grain but a very tiny type of pasta, made from wheat semolina. A Middle Eastern dish made from couscous also bears the same name. Look for it near the rice in your supermarket or in bulk stores.

Marinated Chicken or Turkey Kebabs

Serve kebabs with rice and grilled vegetables such as sweet peppers, zucchini and onion wedges. If desired, serve with Tzatziki (see page 144).

1/4 cup	olive oil 60 mL
2 tbsp	lemon juice 30 mL
1	clove garlic, minced 1
2 tsp	each: minced fresh rosemary and oregano 10 mL
1 tsp	minced fresh thyme or lemon thyme 5 mL
1 lb	boneless skinless chicken or turkey breast 500 g

1. In a medium bowl, whisk together oil, lemon juice, garlic, rosemary, oregano and thyme. Reserve 1 tbsp (15 mL) for brushing on chicken during cooking.
2. Cut chicken into long strips; add to marinade and toss. Cover and refrigerate for 1 to 2 hours.
3. Thread chicken onto skewers. (If using wooden skewers, soak them in water for 30 minutes before using.)
4. Grill over medium-high heat on barbecue for 3 minutes on each side. Brush with reserved marinade. (Or broil in oven about 5 inches/10 cm from heat.)

Makes 4 servings.

Variation
Use 1 tbsp (15 mL) minced fresh cilantro instead of the other herbs.

Roasted Garlic Stuffing with Sage and Thyme

The mellow taste of roasted garlic updates this traditional herbed bread stuffing. It can be cooked separately in a casserole dish or used to stuff a 3-lb (1.5 kg) chicken. To cook with turkey breast, mound stuffing in a baking dish and place breast on top; cover with foil.

2 tbsp	butter 30 mL
1	medium onion, chopped 1
1	stalk celery, chopped 1
1	whole head of roasted garlic* 1
4 cups	dry bread cubes 1 L
1	tart apple, peeled and chopped 1
2 tbsp	each: chopped fresh parsley and sage 30 mL
1 tbsp	chopped fresh thyme 15 mL
1/4 to 1/2 cup	chicken stock or apple juice 60 to 125 mL
	Salt and pepper

1. In a non-stick skillet over medium heat, melt butter. Add onion and celery; cook for 7 minutes or until softened. Stir in roasted garlic; cook for 1 minute.
2. In a 6- to 8-cup (1.5 to 2 L) baking dish, combine bread cubes, apple, parsley, sage, thyme and onion mixture. Pour in enough chicken stock to just moisten bread. Season with a little salt and pepper.
3. Cover and bake in a 350°F (180°C) oven for about 25 minutes or until apple is softened and stuffing is heated through.

Makes 4 servings.

Note

Triple this recipe to stuff a 12- to 15-lb (5 to 7 kg) turkey.

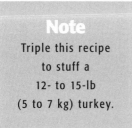

tip

*To roast garlic: Trim about 1/4 inch (5 cm) from the top of a whole head of garlic. Place the garlic head on foil, drizzle with a little olive oil and close foil. Bake in a 325°F (160°C) oven for 50 to 60 minutes or until very soft. Let cool; squeeze softened garlic from papery skins.

Roast Leg of Lamb with Mint Sauce

Herbs, garlic and lamb all seem to go together so well. Serve with Mint Sauce, fluffy mashed potatoes, baby carrots and green beans.

4 lb	leg of lamb (bone-in, short shank) 2 kg
3 or 4	cloves garlic, slivered 3 or 4
2 tbsp	olive oil 30 mL
1 tbsp	lemon juice 15 mL
2 tbsp	finely chopped fresh rosemary 30 mL
2 tsp	finely chopped fresh thyme or lemon thyme 10 mL
1/4 cup	fresh lavender flowers 60 mL (or 1 tbsp/15 mL dried lavender), optional
	Salt and pepper

1. Remove outer membrane from lamb. Using the tip of a sharp knife, make small slits all over lamb; insert garlic slivers.

2. In a small bowl, mix together oil, lemon juice, rosemary, thyme, lavender (if using) and a little salt and pepper. Brush over lamb; place in a glass baking dish. Cover and refrigerate for about 8 hours, or up to 24 hours.

3. Place lamb in a shallow roasting pan; let stand for 30 minutes at room temperature.

4. Roast in a 425°F (220°C) oven for about 15 minutes; reduce heat to 350°F (180°C) for 1 to 1-1/2 hours or until lamb has reached internal temperature of 130°F (54°C) for rare, or 140°F (60°C) for medium-rare (insert thermometer in thickest part of lamb).

5. Transfer to a cutting board; cover loosely with foil and let rest for 10 minutes before slicing. Serve with Mint Sauce (recipe follows).

Makes 6 servings.

Variation
Use 2 tbsp (30 mL) Herbes de Provence (see page 3) instead of fresh herbs.

Mint Sauce

1 cup	finely chopped fresh mint 250 mL
2 tbsp	granulated sugar (or icing or brown sugar) 30 mL
1/4 cup	vinegar (white or red wine cider, malt or balsamic) 60 mL

1. In a medium bowl, place mint; add sugar and stir to crush leaves against the sugar.
2. In a small saucepan over high heat, heat vinegar. Bring to a boil; stir into mint until sugar is dissolved. Let stand for 1 hour. Store in refrigerator for up to 1 week.

Makes about 1/2 cup (125 mL).

Variation
Mint-Cilantro Sauce:
Replace half of the mint
with finely chopped
fresh cilantro.

Oven-Baked Pork Tenderloins

Whole pork tenderloins are marinated in a garlicky mustard and herb baste, then baked. They make an attractive presentation laid overlapping on the plate, garnished with fresh rosemary sprigs. Serve with mashed potatoes or a wild rice blend and green beans, Brussels sprouts or carrots.

2	pork tenderloins (about 3/4 lb/375 g each)	2
2	cloves garlic	2
1 tbsp	each: finely chopped fresh sage (or savory), thyme and rosemary	15 mL
2 tbsp	Dijon mustard	30 mL
1 tbsp	oil	15 mL
2 tsp	coarsely ground pepper	10 mL
1/4 tsp	salt	1 mL

1. Trim any fat from tenderloins; tuck ends under and tie with kitchen cord. Place on large piece of plastic wrap.

2. In food processor, place garlic, sage, thyme and rosemary; pulse until finely chopped. Add mustard, oil, pepper and salt. Purée until smooth, scraping down sides with a spatula. Brush generously over tenderloins. Cover with plastic wrap; refrigerate for about 1 hour.

3. Unwrap tenderloins; place in a shallow roasting pan. Roast in a 400°F (200°C) oven for 25 to 30 minutes, or until meat thermometer inserted in center registers 160°F (70°C).

4. Remove tenderloins to cutting board; tent loosely with foil and let stand for 10 minutes. Remove string; slice thinly on the diagonal.

Makes 4 servings.

Pork Tenderloin Medallions

Pork tenderloin is a tender cut that needs little cooking time. In this recipe, thin slices are coated with a creamy Dijon and rosemary sauce.

2	pork tenderloins (about 2 lb/1 kg total weight) 2
1/4 cup	all-purpose flour 60 mL
1/4 tsp	each: salt and pepper 1 mL
4 tsp	butter or olive oil 20 mL
1/2 cup	chopped shallots 125 mL
1	clove garlic, minced 1
1 cup	chicken stock or dry white wine (or half stock and half wine) 250 mL
2 tbsp	Dijon mustard 30 mL
2 tsp	minced fresh rosemary or Herbes de Provence (see page 3) 10 mL
3 tbsp	18% cream 45 mL
2 tbsp	finely chopped fresh parsley 30 mL

1. Cut tenderloins into slices 3/4 inch (2 cm) thick. Place between waxed paper; pound to 1/4-inch (5 mm) thickness.

2. In a medium bowl, mix together flour, salt and pepper. Dip each medallion to coat; shake off excess.

3. In a large skillet over medium-high heat, melt butter. Add medallions; cook on each side until lightly browned, about 2 minutes per side. Remove to a plate.

4. Using additional butter or oil if necessary, cook shallots and garlic for 2 to 3 minutes or until softened. Add stock; cook, stirring to scrape browned bits from the bottom of the pan, for 1 to 2 minutes. Stir in mustard and rosemary.

5. Return medallions and juices to skillet. Reduce heat; cover and simmer for about 5 minutes.

6. Stir in cream and parsley. Cook for 1 minute to heat through.

Makes 4 servings.

Fried Sage Leaves

Serve with pork, chicken or turkey as a crunchy, edible garnish, or to garnish an hors d'oeuvres platter.

1/2 cup oil (such as sunflower or
canola) 125 mL

Large sage leaves

Seasoning salt, optional

1. In a large skillet over medium-high heat, heat oil until a drop of water sizzles when dropped in.
2. Test one sage leaf; fry for 10 to 15 seconds or until it shrivels slightly. Remove; drain on a paper towel. Once cool, test for crispness. If soft, add another 5 seconds to cooking time. Fry remaining sage leaves, several at a time.
3. Sprinkle with seasoning salt, if using. Serve immediately.

Variation
Fried Parsley: Use same method as above to fry large clumps of curly parsley. Serve with deep-fried camembert or Brie, or as a crispy garnish for soups and meats or fish/seafood dishes.

Broiled Snapper with Lemon and Tarragon Butter

Here's a super-easy fish dish that cooks up quickly under the broiler. Try using sole, tilapia or haddock fillets instead of red snapper. Serve with rice and green beans, broccoli or peas, and carrots.

4	red snapper fillets (about 8 oz/250 g each) 4
2 tbsp	melted butter 30 mL
1 tbsp	minced shallots 15 mL
1 tbsp	finely chopped fresh parsley 15 mL
2 tsp	finely chopped fresh tarragon 10 mL
2 tsp	finely grated lemon rind 10 mL
1 tsp	lemon juice 5 mL
	Tarragon sprigs and lemon slices, for garnish

1. Rinse fish and pat dry with a paper towel. Place on a baking sheet that has been lined with foil and then lightly oiled.

2. In a small bowl, mix together butter, shallots, parsley, tarragon, lemon rind and juice; brush over fish.

3. Place fish under pre-heated broiler about 2 inches (5 cm) from heat. Broil for about 5 minutes, or until fish flakes with fork. To serve, garnish with tarragon sprigs and lemon slices.

Makes 4 servings.

Variation
Use about 3 tbsp (45 mL) prepared herb butters (melted) in place of melted butter, shallots, herbs, lemon rind and juice (see "Herb Butters," page 29).

Herb-Stuffed Trout

A whole trout or salmon is stuffed full of herbs, garlic and lemon. Use individual herbs such as cilantro, dill, lemon basil or tarragon, or a combination such as basil/tarragon, rosemary/lemon thyme or rosemary/oregano.

4	whole rainbow trout(10 to 12 oz/280 to 340 g each) 4 (or 1 whole salmon, about 3 to 4 lb/1.5 to 2 kg)
1 tbsp	lemon juice or white wine 15 mL
1 tbsp	butter or olive oil 15 mL
1	clove garlic, minced 1
1/4 cup	chopped fresh chives 60 mL
4	6-inch (15 cm) sprigs fresh basil 4
4	6-inch (15 cm) sprigs fresh tarragon 4

1. Cut 3 or 4 diagonal slashes on both sides of fish. Place each fish in center of a piece of foil large enough to fold over. Inside fish cavity, sprinkle each fish with one-quarter of each of the lemon juice, butter, garlic and chives. Place one sprig of each herb inside each fish; measure fish at thickest part. Fold foil over fish to seal.

2. Place on barbecue grill over high heat; close lid. Cook for 10 to 12 minutes per inch (4 to 5 minutes per cm) of stuffed thickness (measured at the thickest part), turning once. To check for doneness, open foil and look into slashes. Fish is done when flesh has just become opaque and flakes easily.

   To oven bake: Place wrapped fish on baking sheet. Bake in a 450°F (230°C) oven for 20 to 25 minutes for trout; up to 30 minutes for salmon.

3. Unwrap fish; remove head and tail, cut skin along spine. Fold fish back from center of cavity; discard herbs. Remove spine and bones in one piece. Remove skin if desired. May be served hot or cold.

Makes 4 servings.

Pesto Shrimp

This pesto shrimp was once described by a colleague as the "little black dress" of dishes, it is so simple and so good. May be served as an appetizer with fresh baguette, or as a main course with rice or pasta.

1/2 cup	Basil Pesto (see page 141) 125 mL
1 lb	large shrimp, peeled and deveined 500 g
1/3 cup	white wine 75 mL
1 tsp	lemon juice 5 mL

1. In a large skillet, heat pesto over medium-high heat. Add shrimp, wine and lemon juice; cook, stirring, for 2 to 3 minutes, until the shrimp just turns pink. Serve immediately.

Makes 4 main course or 6 to 8 appetizer servings.

Salmon with Dill Sauce

This sauce is the perfect accompaniment for grilled fish such as salmon, tuna, halibut, swordfish or shark. For a lower-fat sauce, use low-fat sour cream or yogurt and low-fat mayonnaise.

1/2 cup	sour cream or plain yogurt 125 mL
1/2 cup	mayonnaise 125 mL
1 tbsp	finely chopped dill 15 mL
1 tsp	Dijon or Herb Mustard (see page 27) 5 mL
3 tsp	lime juice 15 mL
4	salmon fillets, each about 4 to 6 oz (125 to 175 g) 4
	Salt and pepper, to taste
2 tbsp	oil 30 mL
	Dill sprigs, for garnish

1. In a small bowl, mix together sour cream, mayonnaise, dill, mustard and 1 tsp (5 mL) of the lime juice. Cover and refrigerate until ready to serve.

2. Place salmon, skin side down, on a plate. Sprinkle with remaining 2 tsp (10 mL) of the lime juice. Let stand for about 5 minutes. Season well with salt and pepper.

3. In a large skillet or grill pan over medium-high heat, heat oil. Place salmon in pan, skin side down. Cook for 3 to 5 minutes. Carefully turn over; remove skin. Cook on all sides for 3 to 5 minutes or until salmon is lightly browned and flakes. (Check the thickest part to see if salmon is opaque and flakes.)

   To barbecue: Place salmon, skin side down, on oiled barbecue grill. Brush generously with oil. Cook on all sides over medium-high heat with lid down, and do not remove skin until salmon is completely cooked.

4. To serve, place salmon on individual serving plates. Garnish with dill sprigs. Place about 1/4 cup (60 mL) of the sauce beside the salmon on each plate.

Makes 4 servings.

Variation

Use 2 tsp (10 mL) finely chopped tarragon in place of dill.

Shrimp with Marjoram and Orange

These shrimp have the delightful taste of herbs and orange. Serve hot or cold.

2 tbsp	olive oil 30 mL
1 lb	large shrimp, peeled and deveined 500 g
1	clove garlic, minced 1
2 tsp	finely grated orange rind 10 mL
1/2 cup	orange juice 125 mL
1 tbsp	finely chopped fresh marjoram or oregano 15 mL
1 tbsp	finely chopped fresh parsley 15 mL
1 tbsp	finely chopped marigold petals, optional 15 mL (see "Edible Flowers," page 38)
	Salt and pepper, to taste

1. In a large skillet over medium-high heat, heat oil. Add shrimp and garlic; cook, stirring often, for 1 or 2 minutes, just until shrimp turns pink.
2. Add orange rind and juice; bring to a boil. Cook, stirring, for 1 or 2 minutes or until juice thickens slightly.
3. Stir in marjoram, parsley and marigold petals (if using); season with salt and pepper.

Makes 4 servings.

Variation

Instead of oil, use 2 tbsp (30 mL) Herb Butter (see page 29); replace orange rind and juice with 2 tsp (10 mL) lemon juice and omit other herbs.

Note

Marigolds add a peppery flavor to this dish.

Devilled (Stuffed) Eggs

Most people love to eat stuffed eggs but seldom make them. Take these interesting versions to a party and you'll have a hit. Stuffed eggs are a nutritious snack to have on hand for after school or work and on weekends. Egg yolks are rich in vitamins and minerals, including vitamin A.

6	hard-cooked eggs, peeled and cut in half lengthwise 6
3 tbsp	mayonnaise 45 mL
1 tsp	Dijon mustard or Herb Mustard (see page 27) 5 mL
1 tbsp	minced chives 15 mL
1 tsp	minced fresh tarragon 5 mL (or 2 tsp/10 mL minced fresh dill)
	Salt and pepper, to taste
	Parsley or chive florets, for garnish

1. In a medium bowl, mash egg yolks with a fork. Stir in mayonnaise, mustard, chives, tarragon and a little salt and pepper. (If the mixture is not moist enough, add a little more mayonnaise to desired consistency.)
2. Refill egg whites with yolk filling, using small spoons or a pastry bag fitted with a star tip. Garnish with parsley or chive florets. Serve immediately, or cover and refrigerate for up to 2 days.

Makes 12.

tip

A little herb vinegar (chive, chive flower, purple basil or tarragon) may be added to taste.

Variations

Salmon and Shrimp: Add 2 tbsp (30 mL) mashed smoked salmon or finely chopped cooked shrimp; use dill instead of tarragon. Garnish eggs with small shrimp and/or dill sprigs.

Sun-Dried Tomato and Basil: Add 1 tbsp (15 mL) minced sun-dried tomatoes and use 1 tbsp (15 mL) minced fresh basil instead of the chives and tarragon. Garnish with small basil sprigs.

Olive and Lemon Thyme: Add 1 tbsp (15 mL) minced, pitted Kalamata olives and 1/2 tsp (2 mL) minced fresh lemon thyme (or 1/4 tsp/1 mL minced fresh thyme).

Olive and Sun-Dried Tomato: Add 2 tbsp (30 mL) Olive and Sun-Dried Tomato Tapenade (see page 64). Garnish with small sprigs of fresh parsley.

Egg Salad

This egg salad has a subtle touch of herbs—a nice change from the old stand-by.

4	hard-cooked eggs, peeled 4
2 tbsp	mayonnaise 30 mL
1 tbsp	finely chopped chives 15 mL
1 tsp	minced fresh tarragon or chervil 5 mL
1 tsp	vinegar or tarragon vinegar (see Herb Vinegars, page 19) 5 mL
	Salt and pepper, to taste
2	croissants 2
	Lettuce leaves

1. In a medium bowl, chop eggs using a pastry blender or fork.
2. Stir in mayonnaise, chives, tarragon and vinegar; mix until well combined. Season with salt and pepper.
3. Serve on buttered croissant with a few lettuce leaves.

Makes 2 servings.

tip

Use older eggs rather than fresh for hard-cooking (simmer, do not boil eggs) as they will peel more easily. Crack egg shells all over, roll eggs between hands. Begin peeling from the rounder end.

Herb-Baked Eggs

Treat yourself to a lingering Sunday morning breakfast; sip coffee or juice while you read the paper and let the eggs bake.

2	eggs 2
1 tbsp	each: finely chopped fresh basil and parsley 15 mL
1 tbsp	snipped fresh chives 15 mL
1 tsp	finely chopped fresh tarragon 5 mL
1 tsp	chopped fresh chervil, optional 5 mL
2 tbsp	whipping cream (35%) 30 mL
2 tbsp	shredded Gruyère cheese, or freshly grated Parmesan cheese 30 mL
	Salt and pepper, to taste

1. Butter a 7-inch (18 cm) baking dish. Break eggs into dish; top with basil, parsley, chives, tarragon and chervil (if using). Drizzle with cream.
2. Bake in a 350°F (180°C) oven for about 7 minutes. Sprinkle with cheese. Bake for 3 to 5 minutes longer or until yolks are set to your liking. Season with salt and pepper. Serve immediately.

Makes 1 serving.

Note
Gruyère cheese has a lovely nutty flavor that goes well with herbs.

Scrambled Eggs with Herbs

In mid-summer, when herbs are abundant, my friend Sonja likes to make these quick and easy eggs. Sometimes she adds cheese or a little salsa and fresh cilantro for a taste variation.

2	eggs	2
1 tbsp	milk	15 mL
2 tsp	each: finely chopped fresh parsley and chives	10 mL
1 tsp	chopped fresh tarragon	5 mL
2 tbsp	shredded Gruyère or Cheddar cheese, optional	30 mL
	Salt and pepper	
2 tsp	butter	10 mL

1. In a small bowl, beat together eggs and milk.
2. Stir in parsley, chives, tarragon and cheese (if using). Season with a little salt and pepper.
3. In a small skillet over medium-high heat, melt butter. Pour in egg mixture; cook, stirring often, until eggs begin to set. Serve immediately.

Makes 1 serving.

Variations

- Use 2 tsp (10 mL) finely chopped fresh basil and 1 tsp (5 mL) each: chives, marjoram and parsley in place of other herbs.
- Use 2 tsp (10 mL) each: finely chopped fresh chives and dill in place of other herbs.
- Use 1 tsp (5 mL) each: finely chopped fresh chervil, chives, parsley and tarragon in place of other herbs.
- Use 1 tsp (5 mL) each: finely chopped fresh thyme and parsley in place of other herbs.

Smoked Salmon Strata with Cream Cheese and Dill

This elegant strata is the perfect make-ahead brunch dish.

6	slices Texas toast bread (or thickly sliced white bread) 6
2 tbsp	butter, softened 30 mL
5 ounces	smoked salmon 150 g
1 cup	chopped red onion 250 mL
1	pkg (4 oz/125 g) cream cheese, cut into small cubes 1
4 cups	3/4-inch (2 cm) cubes of Texas toast bread (or cubes of thickly sliced white bread) 1 L
6	eggs 6
2 cups	milk 500 mL
2 tbsp	chopped fresh dill 30 mL
2 tbsp	butter, melted 30 mL
1/4 tsp	salt 1 mL
	Pepper

1. Spread bread slices with about 1 tbsp (15 mL) of the softened butter and place them, buttered side down, in 13- × 9-inch (33 × 23 cm) baking pan (trim to fit if necessary).
2. Place salmon slices in a single layer over bread.
3. In a large skillet over medium heat, melt remaining 1 tbsp (15 mL) of the softened butter. Add onions; cook, stirring, until softened; distribute over salmon. Dot salmon with cream cheese cubes. Top with bread cubes.
4. In a large bowl, whisk together eggs, milk, dill and melted butter. Season with salt and a little pepper. Pour over strata, moistening all the bread cubes. Cover and refrigerate for 4 hours or overnight.
5. Bake in a 350°F (180°C) oven for 35 to 40 minutes, or until puffy and golden. Serve immediately.

Makes 6 to 8 servings.

Vegetable Strata

A strata is a layered egg dish made with dry bread cubes and savory ingredients. This one is full of tasty veggies and cheese—perfect for brunch, a weekend lunch or a casual dinner. It's also wholesome vegetarian fare.

1 tbsp	olive oil 15 mL
1	medium onion, diced 1
1	clove garlic, minced 1
1	small zucchini, diced 1
1/2 lb	mushrooms, sliced 250 g
1	can (28 oz/796 mL) tomatoes, well drained and chopped 1
1/2 cup	diced roasted red pepper 125 mL
2 tbsp	chopped fresh basil 30 mL
	Salt and pepper
4	eggs 4
2 cups	milk 500 mL
6 cups	firm bread cubes (1/2 inch/1 cm thick) 1.5 L
1 cup	shredded mozzarella cheese (about 4 oz/125 g) 250 mL
3 tbsp	grated Parmesan cheese 45 mL

1. In a large non-stick skillet over medium heat, heat oil. Add onion; cook for 5 minutes, stirring occasionally.
2. Stir in garlic, zucchini and mushrooms; cook for 5 minutes, stirring occasionally.
3. Stir in tomatoes, red pepper and basil. Cook for 1 minute or until thickened. Season with a little salt and pepper.
4. In a large bowl, whisk together eggs and milk; set aside.
5. Spoon one-third of the tomato sauce into lightly greased 9-inch (23 cm) square baking pan. Sprinkle with half of the bread cubes; top with another one-third of the sauce and half of the mozzarella, then repeat with remaining bread cubes, sauce and mozzarella.
6. Pour in egg mixture. Sprinkle with Parmesan; cover and refrigerate for about 3 hours or overnight.
7. Bake in a 350°F (180°C) oven for about 40 minutes or until puffed and golden brown. Let stand for 10 minutes before serving.

Makes 6 servings.

Wild Mushroom Frittata

A frittata is an Italian omelette in which the filling ingredients are mixed with the eggs before cooking. It is always served flat rather than folded. Try making one to use up leftovers or cooked vegetables such as asparagus, zucchini, sweet peppers, etc. If you are a mushroom connoisseur, you will enjoy this rendition accented with fresh herbs.

2 tbsp	butter or olive oil (or half of each) 30 mL
1/2 lb	fresh mixed wild mushrooms (shiitake, enoki, criemini), sliced 250 g
1/2 lb	button mushrooms, sliced 250 g
2 tbsp	each: finely chopped fresh parsley and thyme 30 mL
6	eggs 6
1/4 cup	grated Parmesan cheese 60 mL
1/2 cup	shredded Gruyère cheese 125 mL

1. In a large non-stick skillet over medium heat, heat butter. Add wild and button mushrooms; cook for about 5 minutes or until soft and lightly browned. Stir in parsley and thyme; cook for 1 minute.

2. In a medium bowl, beat eggs; stir in Parmesan cheese. Pour over mushrooms in skillet. Lift around the cooked edges with a spatula during the first 2 minutes, to allow uncooked egg to flow underneath. Cover; cook for 3 or 4 more minutes, or until eggs are almost set. Sprinkle with Gruyère cheese.

3. If the skillet is not oven-proof, cover the handle with foil. Put skillet under broiler; broil for 1 or 2 minutes or until cheese melts. To serve, cut into wedges.

Makes 4 servings.

Let the side dish be the star! Add a herbal touch to meats, seafood and eggs in these hot or cold protein partners. Serve creamy dill sauce with grilled salmon, serve rosemary applesauce with roast pork, add a pesto pizzazz to recipes throughout the book and serve cucumber raita as a cooling condiment to spicy Indian dishes.

PESTO, SAUCES AND SALSAS

Recipes

All About Pesto

Traditional basil pesto originated in Genoa, Italy, and is now renowned the world over. Its name comes from the word "pestare," which means to pound or grind. It can be made in the food processor, but traditionalists still make it using a mortar and pestle.

Typically made using large-leaf basil, this delicious and versatile paste can be used with vegetables (especially tomatoes, eggplant and zucchini), with meats and seafood, in soups and cheese spreads, in breads, etc. Refer to the index for many uses of pesto throughout the book.

Ideas for Using Pesto

- toss on hot cooked pasta; add to cheese filling for lasagna
- mix equal parts with sour cream or plain yogurt for a veggie dip
- spoon onto a baked potato and top with extra Parmesan cheese
- stir into mashed potatoes along with a bit of warmed milk
- spread on crackers or toasted bread
- spread on toasted bread and cover with sliced tomatoes
- Bruschetta: rub bread with garlic, brush with olive oil, top with pesto and fresh diced tomatoes
- halve beefsteak tomatoes, place 1 tbsp (15 mL) pesto on each and let marinate for an hour; sprinkle with Parmesan cheese; eat cold or broil
- halve an eggplant and bake until almost soft; make slices 1 inch (2.5 cm) apart and several inches deep but not all the way through; spread with pesto, sprinkle with thinly sliced Parmesan cheese and bake until cheese is melted and golden
- add to mayonnaise or sour cream and use as a sandwich spread, a dressing for seafood or pasta salads or potato salads, a dip or a topping for a baked potato
- spread on the bottom crust for a tomato tart, tomato quiche or pizza
- add a dollop to omelettes or frittata
- stir into a finished risotto

continued…

- stir a spoonful into a vinaigrette for salad, or into dressing for grilled vegetables, bean salads
- stir into a vegetable stew (onions, garlic, sweet green and red peppers, zucchini, tomatoes, potatoes)
- stir into soups such as minestrone, zucchini, lentil
- serve a dollop with grilled foods such as chicken or fish
- marinate chicken or lamb in 2 tbsp (30 mL) pesto, 1 tbsp (15 mL) lemon juice and pepper; marinate about 2 hours; brush on additional marinade when grilling or broiling
- brush on refrigerator crescent rolls, roll up and bake
- brush on puff pastry strips, twist and bake
- use to fill mushroom caps, top with breadcrumbs and bake

Substitutions

- In place of pine nuts, use pistachios (unsalted, roasted), cashews, walnuts, pecans, sunflower seeds, blanched almonds. To enhance their flavor, toast in a 325°F (160°C) oven for about 8 minutes; cool to room temperature before adding.
- For a lower-fat version, reduce the oil to 1/4 cup (60 mL) and add 2 tsp (10 mL) lemon juice and 1/2 cup (125 mL) chicken stock. Use right away.
- Replace some of the oil with the oil from sun-dried tomatoes.
- Use sunflower oil in place of olive oil.
- Use 1/4 cup (60 mL) grated Pecorino Romano cheese, 1/4 cup (60 mL) grated Parmigiano Reggiano cheese.
- Roast garlic. Wrap about 8 unpeeled garlic cloves in foil wrap; roast in a 425°F (220°C) oven about 25 minutes or until very soft. Unwrap, cool to room temperature; squeeze garlic from cloves.

Basil Pesto

2 cups	packed basil leaves	500 mL
1/4 cup	Italian parsley leaves (or 1/2 cup/125 mL curly parsley), optional	60 mL
3	cloves garlic	3
1/2 cup	pine nuts	125 mL
1/2 cup	grated Parmesan cheese (use Parmigiano Reggiano)	125 mL
1/3 to 1/2 cup	olive oil	75 to 125 mL

1. In food processor, combine basil, parsley (if using), garlic and pine nuts; pulse until finely minced.
2. Add cheese and process to blend.
3. Using the feed tube, slowly drizzle in oil, processing to a moist paste.
4. Remove to a small bowl and cover with plastic wrap pressed onto the surface. (This prevents oxidative browning.) Or cover surface with a thin film of oil, or place pesto in a medium zip-lock bag, remove air and seal. Pesto will keep, refrigerated, for about a week.

Makes about 1-1/2 cups (375 mL).

tip

Tips for Thawing: To perk up the color after thawing, stir in 2 tbsp (30 mL) chopped fresh parsley. Thaw in refrigerator. Do not use microwave to thaw, as it can cook the pesto.

Note

To freeze pesto, prepare as above, omitting cheese and using the smaller amount of oil. Place in a freezer container covered with a thin film of oil or freeze in a zip-lock freezer bag. Cheese can be stirred in after thawing. Use ice cube trays to freeze small amounts of pesto; once frozen remove to freezer bag, label and date. May be kept frozen for several months.

Raita (Cucumber-Yogurt Sauce)

This condiment is a great complement to the heat of spicy Indian dishes.

1 cup	plain yogurt 250 mL
1/2 cup	diced peeled English cucumber (or peeled and seeded field cucumber) 125 mL
1/4 cup	chopped green onions or sweet onion 60 mL
2 tbsp	liquid honey 30 mL
2 tbsp	finely chopped fresh cilantro 30 mL (or 1 tbsp/15 mL finely chopped fresh mint)
pinch	each: salt and ground cumin pinch

1. In a medium bowl, mix together all ingredients. Refrigerate for up to 2 days. If making ahead, sprinkle chopped cucumber with salt; let stand for 5 minutes. Rinse and drain; then add to yogurt.

Makes about 1 cup (250 mL).

Variation
Add diced, peeled apple or finely grated carrot instead of cucumber.

Rosemary Applesauce

Serve this sweet sauce with pork roast or pork chops. Use apples that soften when they cook, such as McIntosh, Empire, Cortland, Golden Delicious or Russet.

2	large, tart apples, peeled, cored and sliced (about 3 cups/750 mL)	2
3	3-inch (7.5 cm) sprigs fresh rosemary	3
2 tbsp	pure maple syrup or brown sugar, optional	30 mL

1. In a 4-cup (1 L) glass measuring cup, gently mix together apples and rosemary sprigs. Cover with plastic wrap; microwave on high for 3 to 6 minutes, stirring occasionally, until apples are very soft. Let stand until cool.

2. Remove rosemary; discard. Stir until apples are smooth. Stir in maple syrup (if using).

Makes 1 cup (250 mL).

Variation
Use fresh sage leaves instead of rosemary.

Tzatziki (Mint-Cucumber Dip)

This garlicky Greek dip can be served with warmed pita bread or raw vegetables. It may also be served over sliced tomatoes or to top burgers.

2 cups	plain yogurt 500 mL
3/4 cup	finely grated, peeled and seeded cucumber 175 mL
2	cloves garlic, crushed 2
1 tsp	lemon juice 5 mL
1 tbsp	finely chopped fresh mint 15 mL
2 tbsp	finely chopped fresh dill, optional 30 mL
	Salt and pepper, to taste

1. Place yogurt in a coffee filter or wet paper towel set into a sieve over a bowl. Cover and refrigerate for about 3 hours, until some of the liquid drains off and yogurt thickens slightly.
2. Sprinkle cucumber with a little salt. Let stand for 5 minutes; pour through sieve and squeeze to remove liquid.
3. In a medium bowl, mix together thickened yogurt, cucumber, garlic, lemon juice, mint and dill (if using). Season with a little salt and pepper.

Makes about 1-1/2 cups (375 mL).

tip

To crush garlic, finely chop it and sprinkle with salt. Use the side of a knife blade to mash it into a paste. Remember to reduce the amount of salt in your recipe.

Salsas

Tomato salsa currently outsells ketchup in North America as the hottest appetizer/condiment going, no doubt because it's low in fat and has spice-appeal. Today salsa can mean anything from fruity concoctions nestled alongside grilled foods to fresh or cooked tortilla dips, but all have one thing in common—the addition of chili peppers.

Choose your hot peppers wisely; most available are jalapeños and red finger hots, but if you think the hotter, the better, then go for the fiery blaze of Jamaican, habaneros or Scotch bonnets.

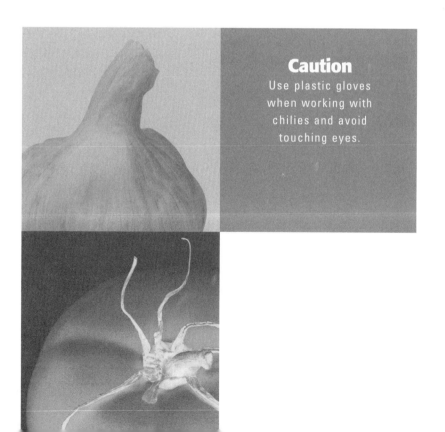

Caution
Use plastic gloves when working with chilies and avoid touching eyes.

Black Bean and Corn Salsa

Feel free to turn up the heat by using some of the scorching varieties of chili peppers out there. This makes a great little side salad to chicken or ribs, a delicious topping for tacos or great dip for nachos.

1 cup	cooked black beans, drained 250 mL
1 cup	cooked kernel corn 250 mL
1 cup	chopped, seeded tomatoes 250 mL
1/3 cup	diced sweet onion or green onion 75 mL
1/4 cup	diced roasted red peppers 60 mL
1 tbsp	minced jalapeño pepper 15 mL
1 tbsp	chopped fresh cilantro or parsley 15 mL
1	large clove garlic, minced 1
	Salt and pepper, to taste

1. In a large bowl combine all ingredients, stirring gently to mix well. May be made ahead and refrigerated up to 3 days.

Makes about 3-1/2 cups (875 mL).

Mango Pineapple Salsa

Serve this salsa with grilled chicken, or fish such as swordfish, shark and tuna.

3/4 cup	diced mango, peach or papaya 175 mL
3/4 cup	diced pineapple 175 mL
1/2 cup	diced red pepper 125 mL
1/4 cup	chopped green onion 60 mL
2 tbsp	minced jalapeño pepper, or to taste 30 mL
2 tbsp	chopped fresh cilantro 30 mL
2 tsp	lime juice 10 mL
1/4 tsp	ground cumin 1 mL

1. In a medium bowl, combine all ingredients. Let stand for 30 minutes to allow flavors to develop.

Makes about 2 cups (500 mL).

Variation

Use 1 tbsp (15 mL) finely chopped fresh mint (such as spearmint or pineapple mint) in place of cilantro.

Fresh Tomato Salsa

Make this fresh salsa when tomatoes are at their sweet best. It's a tasty combination that's a great substitute for bruschetta topping.

2 cups	diced, seeded tomatoes 500 mL
2	green onions, chopped 2
1	clove garlic, minced 1
1 tbsp	minced jalapeño pepper 15 mL
1 tbsp	finely chopped fresh cilantro 15 mL
1 tbsp	each: lime juice and olive oil 15 mL
1/4 tsp	ground cumin 1 mL
	Salt and pepper, to taste

1. In a medium bowl combine all ingredients, stirring gently to mix well. For best flavor, do not refrigerate, and use salsa within a few hours of making.

Makes 2 cups (500 mL).

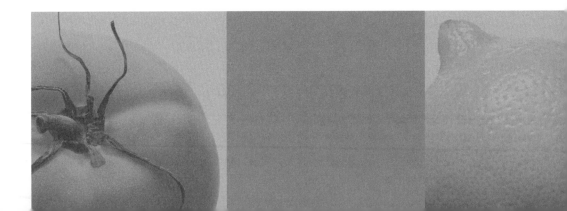

From delicate pasta with lemon and herbs to piquant pesto, rich risotto and hearty grains, herbs add flavors that take these starches to new heights.

PASTA, RICE AND GRAINS

Recipes

Chicken Fettuccine in Pesto-Cream Sauce

Pesto lovers will enjoy this creamy pasta sauce. Substitute shrimp for the chicken, if you like.

8 oz	fettuccine (or linguine or penne) 250 g
1 tbsp	oil 15 mL
2	boneless, skinless chicken breasts, sliced 2
1/2 cup	Basil Pesto (see page 141) 125 mL
1/3 cup	sun-dried tomatoes, sliced or chopped 75 mL
1 cup	18% cream 250 mL
	Parsley sprigs, for garnish
	Freshly grated Parmesan cheese

1. In a large pot of boiling salted water, cook fettuccine until tender but firm.
2. Meanwhile, in a very large skillet over medium heat, heat oil. Add chicken; cook on both sides until lightly browned.
3. Stir in pesto and sun-dried tomatoes; cook until heated through. Add cooked pasta to skillet.
4. Pour in cream; stir gently to coat pasta and heat through. Garnish with parsley and serve immediately with Parmesan.

Makes 2 servings.

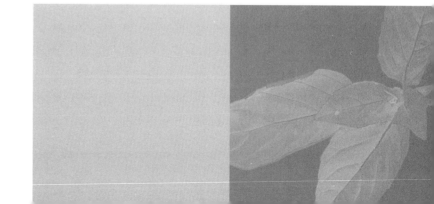

Fresh Tomato and Basil Sauce

Enjoy this delicious fresh sauce with pasta or as a bruschetta topping.

1/4 cup	olive oil 60 mL
1	small onion, chopped 1
2	cloves garlic, minced 2
1-1/2 lb	fresh tomatoes, seeded and chopped 750 g
1/3 cup	drained and chopped sun-dried tomatoes (oil-packed) 75 mL
1/2 cup	coarsely chopped fresh basil 125 mL
1/4 cup	coarsely chopped fresh parsley 60 mL
1/4 tsp	hot red pepper flakes, optional 1 mL
	Salt and pepper, to taste

1. In a large skillet over medium heat, heat oil. Add onion; cook for 5 minutes or until softened. Stir in garlic; cook for 1 minute.
2. Stir in fresh and sun-dried tomatoes. Reduce heat to medium-low; cook for 3 minutes or until fresh tomatoes begin to break down.
3. Stir in basil, parsley and hot red pepper flakes (if using). Cook for 1 minute; season with salt and pepper. Serve over hot rotini or fusilli with freshly grated Parmesan cheese.

Makes 2 large servings or 4 appetizer servings.

Bruschetta

Spread sauce on prepared toasts; top with grated Parmesan and broil for about 2 minutes or until cheese is golden.

Herbed Orzo

This speedy dish is excellent served with grilled chicken or lamb, or as a summer pasta salad with sliced cooked chicken or fish stirred in.

2 cups	orzo pasta 500 mL
2 tbsp	olive oil 30 mL
1	large clove garlic, minced 1 (or 2 tsp/10 mL minced garlic chives)
1/3 cup	finely chopped fresh parsley 75 mL
2 tbsp	finely chopped fresh oregano 30 mL
1 tsp	finely grated lemon rind 5 mL
1/2 cup	crumbled feta cheese 125 mL

1. In a medium saucepan of boiling salted water, cook orzo for 6 to 8 minutes or just until tender. Drain well.

2. In a large skillet over medium-low heat, heat oil. Stir in garlic, parsley, oregano and lemon rind. Cook, stirring, for about 1 minute.

3. Stir in orzo and feta; heat through.

Makes 4 servings.

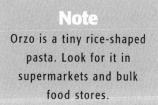

Note

Orzo is a tiny rice-shaped pasta. Look for it in supermarkets and bulk food stores.

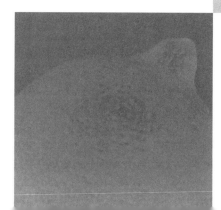

Pad Thai

It is the variety of interesting ingredients that makes this trendy dish so popular. Fresh cilantro gives this dish its final signature.

2 tbsp	each: soy sauce, lemon juice 30 mL
1 tbsp	each: ketchup, packed brown sugar 15 mL
2 tsp	dark sesame oil 10 mL
1/4 tsp	hot red pepper flakes 1 mL
5 oz	wide rice stick noodles 150 g
1 tbsp	oil 15 mL
1	boneless chicken breast, thinly sliced 1
6 oz	extra-firm tofu, cut into 1/2-inch (1 cm) cubes 175 g
2	cloves garlic, minced 2
1 tbsp	minced fresh ginger 15 mL
half	each: sweet red and yellow peppers, thinly sliced half
12	peeled and deveined, cooked jumbo shrimp, optional 12
1 cup	bean sprouts 250 mL
1/4 cup	each: chopped roasted peanuts, sliced green onions, chopped fresh cilantro 60 mL

1. In a small bowl, mix together soy sauce, lemon juice, ketchup, brown sugar, sesame oil and hot red pepper flakes; set aside.
2. Cook noodles in boiling salted water for 2 to 3 minutes or until tender. Drain noodles, cover and set aside.
3. In large wok or non-stick skillet over medium heat, heat oil. Cook chicken just until it changes color; remove with a slotted spoon.
4. Add tofu, garlic and ginger to pan; cook for 1 minute. Stir in peppers; cook for 2 minutes.
5. Stir in shrimp (if using), bean sprouts and cooked noodles. Pour in soy sauce mixture. Toss well and heat through.
6. Serve immediately, sprinkled with peanuts, onion and cilantro.

Makes 4 servings.

Variation

For a meatless version, omit the chicken and replace with 2 eggs. Beat eggs and cook in the center of the wok, after the red peppers are cooked, stirring eggs to scramble. Stir eggs into mixture.

Pasta with Lemon and Herb Cream Sauce

This is a great side dish to serve with grilled shrimp or chicken.

8 oz	spaghetti or linguine	250 g
1 tbsp	olive oil	15 mL
1/2 cup	finely chopped shallots	125 mL
3/4 cup	18% cream	75 mL
1/2 cup	chicken or vegetable stock (or half stock and half white wine)	125 mL
2 tsp	grated lemon rind	10 mL
4 tbsp	finely chopped fresh parsley	60 mL
2 tbsp	snipped fresh chives	30 mL

1. In a large pot of boiling salted water, cook pasta until tender but firm; drain.
2. In a large skillet over medium heat, heat oil. Add shallots; cook, stirring often, for 2 or 3 minutes or until softened.
3. Stir in cream and stock. Simmer, uncovered, until sauce reduces and is slightly thickened, for about 5 minutes.
4. Add pasta, lemon rind, parsley and chives; toss to coat well. Serve immediately.

Makes 2 servings.

Variations

- If serving with fish, add 2 tbsp (30 mL) chopped fresh dill; add 2 tbsp (30 mL) chopped toasted walnuts just before serving.
- Use 2 tbsp (30 mL) finely chopped fresh sage in place of chives. Add 1/2 cup (125 mL) fresh or frozen cooked peas, 3 oz (75 g) diced prosciutto or smoked ham; cook 1 minute longer. Sprinkle with 1/4 cup (60 mL) Parmesan cheese.

Pesto Pasta

The rich herbal aroma of this dish promises a treat for the tastebuds! Savor the crunch of toasted pine nuts, the chewiness and tang of sun-dried tomatoes and the robustness of fresh curls of Parmesan in this speedy pasta. Serve it as the main course with a salad, or as the perfect side dish to roasted chicken. This dish was a big hit at my herb cooking classes.

1 lb	penne (lisce or rigate) 500 g
1 cup (approx.)	Basil Pesto (see page 141) 250 mL
12	cherry tomatoes, halved 12
1/3 cup	chopped sun-dried tomatoes 75 mL
1/4 cup	toasted pine nuts 60 mL
	Pepper, to taste
1/4 cup	shaved Parmesan cheese 60 mL
	Fresh basil leaves, for garnish

1. In a large pot of boiling salted water, cook penne until tender but firm; drain well. Transfer to a heated serving dish.

2. Add pesto to pasta and toss. If pesto is a little too thick to blend in, add 1 tbsp (15 mL) pasta water or hot water.

3. Stir in cherry tomatoes, sun-dried tomatoes and pine nuts; season with pepper.

4. Use a cheese plane or vegetable peeler to make cheese shavings; sprinkle on top of pasta. Garnish top with fresh basil leaves. Serve hot or at room temperature.

Makes 4 to 6 servings.

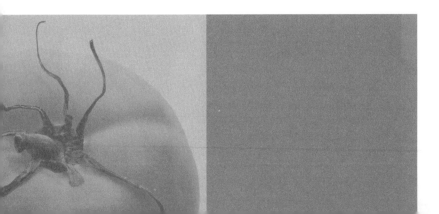

Shrimp, Salmon and Asparagus Pasta Salad

This is a nice, light summer salad that is attractive served on lettuce leaves and garnished with fresh dill sprigs and lemon wedges.

Salad

3 cups	small pasta shells	750 mL
1/2 lb	asparagus (or 6 oz/175 g snow peas, halved diagonally)	250 g
1 cup	each: cooked peeled shrimp and chunks of poached or grilled salmon	250 mL
1/4 cup	chopped red onion	60 mL

Dressing

1/4 cup	low-fat plain yogurt or sour cream	60 mL
2 tbsp	low-fat mayonnaise	30 mL
1 tbsp	lemon juice	15 mL
1	clove garlic, crushed	1
1/4 cup	chopped fresh chives	60 mL
2 tbsp	finely chopped fresh dill	30 mL
	Salt and pepper	
	Leaf lettuce	
	Dill sprigs and lemon wedges, for garnish	

Salad

1. In a large pot of boiling salted water, cook pasta shells until tender but firm. Drain; rinse under cold running water; drain well.
2. Trim asparagus and cut into small pieces. Cook in microwave or in a saucepan of boiling water just until tender-crisp. Immediately drain and cover with cold water until cool; drain well.
3. In a large bowl combine pasta, asparagus, shrimp, salmon and onion.

Dressing

1. In a small bowl, mix together yogurt, mayonnaise, lemon juice and garlic. Stir in chives and dill; add a little salt and pepper. Pour over salad and mix gently. Taste and adjust seasoning.
2. Cover and chill for 1 to 2 hours to blend flavors. Serve on lettuce leaves on individual salad plates; garnish with dill sprigs and lemon wedges.

Makes 4 servings.

Summer Vegetable Pasta

Enjoy the sweet taste of summer's tomatoes with zucchini or summer squash, garlic and a bounty of fresh herbs. Parsley has the ability to soften the taste of other herbs as well as to blend the flavors of mixed herbs with each other and with other ingredients. When using Italian parsley in place of curly parsley less is needed, as it has a stronger flavor.

1 lb	fusilli or rotini	500 g
2 tbsp	olive oil	30 mL
4 cups	diced or chopped zucchini	1 L
1	clove garlic, minced	1
4 cups	chopped tomatoes	1 L
1/4 cup	white wine or dry sherry	60 mL
1/3 cup	chopped fresh basil	75 mL
1/4 cup	chopped fresh chives	60 mL
1/4 cup	chopped fresh Italian parsley	60 mL
2 tbsp	chopped fresh marjoram	30 mL
	Salt and pepper, to taste	
	Grated Parmesan cheese	

1. In a large pot of boiling salted water, cook pasta until tender but firm; drain.
2. Meanwhile, in a large skillet over medium heat, heat oil. Add zucchini and garlic and cook for 5 minutes, stirring frequently.
3. Add tomatoes and wine; cook for 5 minutes, stirring frequently, until sauce thickens. Stir in basil, chives, parsley and marjoram; cook for 2 minutes. Season with salt and pepper.
4. Toss sauce with pasta; serve immediately with Parmesan.

Makes 4 servings.

Arroz Verde (Green Rice)

Serve this tasty rice dish with grilled chicken, fish or baked bean or lentil casseroles. Texmati is a variety of rice grown in the southern United States and is related to Indian basmati rice.

1 cup	Texmati rice 250 mL
2 cups	chicken or vegetable stock 500 mL
1/2 cup	finely chopped fresh cilantro 125 mL
1/4 cup	snipped chives 60 mL
1 tsp	finely grated lime rind, optional 5 mL
1 tbsp	lime juice 15 mL
	Salt and pepper, to taste

1. In a large saucepan over high heat, mix together rice and chicken stock; bring to a boil. Reduce heat; cover and simmer for about 15 minutes or until rice is tender.
2. Remove from heat; stir in cilantro, chives, lime rind (if using) and lime juice. Season with salt and pepper.
3. Cover and let stand for 10 minutes before serving.

Makes 6 servings.

Variation
Use parsley instead of cilantro and stir in 1 to 2 tbsp (15 to 30 mL) finely chopped edible flowers (see "Edible Flowers," page 38.)

Asparagus and Mushroom Risotto with Roasted Garlic

Risotto is a classic, creamy rice dish from Italy, typically made with arborio rice. The rice will be slightly firm in the center when done. Serve with roast pork or chops.

3 tbsp	olive oil 45 mL
1/2 lb	mushrooms, sliced 250 g
1/2 oz	dried porcini mushrooms (re-hydrated in very hot water for 30 minutes) 15 g
3/4 cup	each: diced red onion and diced sweet yellow pepper 175 mL
1 tbsp	finely chopped fresh thyme or lemon thyme 15 mL
1/2 lb	fresh asparagus 250 g
1-1/2 cups	arborio rice 375 mL
1/2 cup	dry white wine 125 mL
6 cups	hot chicken stock 1.5 L
1	whole head roasted garlic (see page 119) 1
3/4 cup	grated Parmesan cheese 175 mL
1/4 cup	chopped fresh Italian parsley 60 mL
	Salt and pepper, to taste

1. In a large skillet over medium-high heat, heat 2 tbsp (30 mL) of the oil. Add sliced mushrooms; cook, stirring frequently, until tender.

2. Drain porcini mushrooms, reserving soaking liquid. Stir porcini mushrooms, onion, yellow pepper and thyme into cooked mushrooms. Cook for about 2 minutes, stirring occasionally; set aside.

3. Cut asparagus tips about 1-1/2 inches (4 cm) long; set aside. Chop stems into 3/4-inch (1.5 cm) pieces. Cook stems in boiling water for 2 minutes; add tips and cook for 1 minute longer; drain and set aside.

4. In a large skillet or wok over high heat, heat remaining 1 tbsp (15 mL) of the oil. Add rice; cook, stirring, for 1 minute. Add wine and reserved liquid from dried mushrooms. Cook, stirring constantly, until liquid is almost completely absorbed. Stir in stock 3/4 cup (175 mL) at a time, stirring constantly, adding more when it is almost completely absorbed. This should take about 20 minutes.

5. Stir in roasted garlic, mushroom mixture, asparagus, 1/2 cup (125 mL) of the Parmesan cheese and parsley. Season with salt and pepper. Sprinkle each serving with remaining 1/4 cup (60 mL) of the Parmesan cheese.

Makes 4 servings.

Risotto Variations

Pesto Risotto

Serve with chicken or veal.

1. In a large skillet over medium-high heat, heat oil. Add 1/2 cup (125 mL) chopped onion; cook until softened, about 7 minutes.

2. Skip to step 4 (omit mushrooms, red onion, yellow pepper, thyme, asparagus and roasted garlic).

3. When rice is creamy and tender, stir in about 1/3 cup (75 mL) Basil Pesto (see page 141) and 1/2 cup (125 mL) Parmesan cheese. Season with salt and pepper. Sprinkle each serving with the remaining cheese.

Rosemary and Asiago Risotto

Serve with lamb, pork, chicken or veal.

1. In a large skillet over medium-high heat, heat oil. Add 1/2 cup (125 mL) chopped onion; cook until softened, about 7 minutes. Stir in 2 minced garlic cloves and 1 tbsp (15 mL) minced fresh rosemary; cook 1 minute longer.

2. Skip to step 4 (omit mushrooms, red onion, yellow pepper, thyme, asparagus and roasted garlic).

3. When rice is creamy and tender, stir in about 1/2 cup (125 mL) grated Asiago cheese and 1/4 cup (60 mL) grated Parmesan cheese. Season with salt and pepper. Sprinkle with 2 tbsp (30 mL) chopped fresh Italian parsley.

Salmon and Tarragon Risotto

1. In a large skillet over medium-high heat, heat oil. Add 1/2 cup (125 mL) chopped shallots; cook until softened, about 7 minutes.

2. Skip to step 4 (omit mushrooms, red onion, yellow pepper, thyme, asparagus and roasted garlic).

3. When rice is creamy and tender, stir in 2 tbsp (30 mL) each: finely chopped fresh parsley and tarragon (or 3 tbsp/45 mL finely chopped fresh dill), 3/4 cup (175 mL) cooked fresh or frozen peas and 1 lb (500 g) chunks of grilled or poached Atlantic salmon (omit Parmesan cheese); heat through. Season with salt and pepper.

Shrimp Risotto

Use 1 lb (500g) grilled, sautéed or poached shrimp in place of salmon in above variation.

Barley and Rice Pilaf

Barley combines with brown and wild rices to give an interesting crunch to this whole-grain pilaf.

2 tbsp	oil	30 mL
1	medium onion, chopped	1
1/3 cup	pot barley	75 mL
1/3 cup	long-grain brown rice	75 mL
1/4 cup	wild rice	60 mL
2 cups	beef, chicken or vegetable stock	500 mL
1/2 lb	mushrooms, chopped	250 g
1	stalk celery, diced	1
1	large carrot, grated	1
2 tsp	chopped fresh thyme	10 mL
1/4 cup	chopped fresh parsley	60 mL
	Salt and pepper, to taste	

1. In a large saucepan over medium heat, heat 1 tbsp (15 mL) of the oil. Add onions and cook for 7 minutes or until soft.
2. Stir in barley, brown and wild rice; cook, stirring, for 1 minute.
3. Add stock; increase heat to high and bring to a boil. Reduce heat; cover and simmer 50 to 60 minutes or until grains are tender.
4. In a Dutch oven over medium heat, heat remaining 1 tbsp (15 mL) of the oil. Stir in mushrooms, celery, carrot and thyme; cook for 5 minutes or until celery is tender. Stir in cooked grains and parsley. Season with salt and pepper.

Makes 6 servings.

Stuffed Sweet Peppers

These tasty peppers are stuffed with a high-fiber mixture of brown rice, lentils and corn. Prepared salsa and canned legumes (peas, beans and lentils) provide extra convenience. Make these as hot or as mild as you like.

4	large sweet green peppers 4
1 tbsp	oil 15 mL
1/2 cup	diced onions 125 mL
1	clove garlic, minced 1
2 cups	cooked brown or white rice 500 mL
3/4 cup	cooked lentils 175 mL
1/2 cup	frozen corn kernels 125 mL
1/3 cup	chopped cilantro 75 mL
1 cup	coarsely shredded Monterey Jack cheese 250 mL
1 cup	mild salsa (or to taste) 250 mL
	Salt and pepper, to taste
8 tbsp	coarsely shredded Monterey Jack cheese 120 mL

1. Cut the tops from the peppers; remove seeds and membranes. Trim bottoms flat so peppers stand up. In a large pot of boiling water, cook peppers for 2 minutes; drain, cut side down, on a paper towel.

2. In a large non-stick skillet over medium heat, heat oil. Add onions; cook for 5 minutes. Add garlic; cook for 1 minute.

3. In a large bowl, mix together onion mixture, rice, lentils, corn and cilantro. Stir in 1 cup (250 mL) of the cheese and salsa. Season with salt and pepper.

4. Fill prepared peppers with rice mixture. Place in an 8-inch (20 cm) square baking dish; add a little water to pan. Cover with foil; bake in a 400°F (200°C) oven for about 25 minutes. Top each pepper with 2 tbsp (30 mL) of the cheese. Return to oven, uncovered, for 5 minutes or until cheese melts.

Makes 4 servings.

Variations
- For extra heat, use hot salsa or add minced jalapeño peppers to rice mixture.
- Substitute black beans for the lentils.
- Substitute Cheddar or mozzarella cheese for the Monterey Jack.

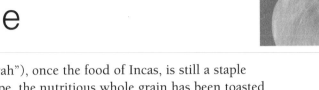

Quinoa and Squash Casserole

Quinoa (pronounced "keen-wah"), once the food of Incas, is still a staple in South America. In this recipe, the nutritious whole grain has been toasted to give it a nutty flavor to go with its slightly crunchy texture.

1 cup	quinoa	250 mL
1 tbsp	oil	15 mL
1/2 cup	diced onion	125 mL
1	clove garlic, minced	1
1 cup	diced butternut squash or carrot	250 mL
1 cup	orange or apple juice	250 mL
1 cup	chicken or vegetable stock	250 mL
1/2 tsp	salt	2 mL
1/4 cup	chopped fresh parsley	60 mL
2 tbsp	chopped fresh marjoram 30 mL (or 1 tbsp/15 mL chopped fresh savory)	

1. Rinse quinoa and drain well. In a large skillet over medium-high heat, cook and stir quinoa until water is gone; reduce heat to medium and continue to stir until toasted. Place toasted quinoa in 2-quart (2 L) baking dish.

2. In a skillet over medium heat, heat oil. Add onion and cook, stirring occasionally, for about 7 minutes or until softened. Add garlic and squash; cook for 2 minutes.

3. Add onion mixture, juice, stock and salt to quinoa in baking dish; stir to combine. Cover and bake in a 375°F (190°C) oven for 30 minutes; remove cover and continue to cook for about 10 minutes longer or until liquid is absorbed and grain and squash are tender.

4. Stir in parsley and marjoram; fluff with fork.

Makes 4 servings.

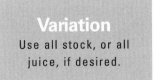

Variation
Use all stock, or all juice, if desired.

*Eat your veggies, in style. What wonders
herbs do for vegetables. Use a touch of
herb butter or vinegar to bring out the best
in vegetables, beans and lentils.
Drizzle with a touch of herbal oil or add
fresh herbs to a sauce.*

VEGETABLES
AND
LEGUMES

Recipes

Vegetable/Herb Chart

This vegetable goes with...	...these herbs
Artichokes	Bay leaves, parsley, sage, tarragon, thyme
Asparagus	Basil, bay leaves, chives, lemon balm, marjoram, parsley, sage, savory, tarragon, thyme
Avocados	Cilantro, dill, marjoram
Beans (green, wax)	Basil, chives, cilantro, dill, marjoram, mint, oregano, parsley, rosemary, sage, savory, tarragon, thyme
Beets	Bay leaves, dill, tarragon
Broccoli	Basil, chives/garlic chives, dill, lemon balm, marjoram, oregano, savory, tarragon, thyme
Brussels sprouts	Marjoram, sage, savory
Cabbage	Dill, oregano, parsley, sage, savory, tarragon
Carrots	Basil, bay leaf, chervil, chives, cilantro, dill, lemon balm, marjoram, mint, oregano, parsley, sage, savory, tarragon, thyme
Cauliflower	Basil, chives/garlic chives, dill, marjoram, parsley, rosemary, savory, tarragon
Celery	Basil, chives, cilantro, marjoram, oregano, parsley, tarragon, thyme
Corn	Basil, chervil, chives, cilantro, lemon balm, marjoram, oregano, parsley, sage, savory, rosemary, thyme
Cucumbers	Chervil, chives, dill, mint, parsley
Eggplant	Basil, bay leaves, chervil, chives, cilantro, marjoram, oregano, parsley, rosemary, sage, savory, thyme
Greens (Kale, collards, Swiss chard, tarragon, dandelion, mustard, etc.)	Marjoram, rosemary, savory

This vegetable goes with...	...these herbs
Leeks	Chives, oregano, parsley, thyme
Mushrooms	Basil, chives, cilantro, marjoram, oregano, parsley, tarragon, thyme
Okra	Dill, oregano, parsley, thyme
Onions	Basil, marjoram, oregano, parsley, sage, tarragon, thyme
Parsnips	Basil, chervil, chives, dill, marjoram, parsley, savory, tarragon, thyme
Peas	Basil, bay leaves, chervil, chives, dill, marjoram, mint, oregano, rosemary, savory, tarragon, thyme
Peppers, sweet	Basil, chives, marjoram, oregano, parsley, thyme
Potatoes	Basil, chives, cilantro, dill, marjoram, mint, oregano, parsley, sage, rosemary, tarragon, thyme
Potatoes, sweet	Parsley, sage, thyme
Spinach	Basil, chervil, chives, dill, marjoram, mint, oregano, rosemary, tarragon, thyme
Squash, summer	Basil, chives, dill, marjoram, oregano, parsley, sage, savory, thyme
Squash, winter	Parsley, rosemary, sage
Tomatoes	Basil, bay leaf, chives/garlic chives, cilantro, dill, marjoram, oregano, parsley, sage, savory, tarragon, thyme
Turnip	Basil, chives, dill, marjoram, parsley, rosemary, sage, savory

Baby Carrots in Dill-Chive Cream Sauce

Not at all like the flavor of dill pickles, fresh dill leaves have a delicate, fresh taste. Save a few pretty dill sprigs for garnish. Chives are a convenient way to add a subtle onion essence. This dish will nicely complement chicken or fish.

1 lb	baby carrots 500 g
2 tbsp	butter 30 mL
1 tbsp	all-purpose flour 15 mL
1/3 cup	each: chicken or vegetable stock and light cream 75 mL
1 tbsp	finely chopped fresh dill 15 mL
1 tbsp	snipped fresh chives 15 mL
	Salt

1. Cook carrots whole in boiling water just until tender; drain well.
2. In a small saucepan over medium heat, melt butter. Whisk in flour; cook for 1 minute, stirring constantly.
3. Stir in stock; bring to a boil, stirring frequently until sauce thickens.
4. Stir in cream; cook for about 1 minute.
5. Stir in dill and chives. Pour over hot carrots; toss to coat. Season with a little salt.

Makes 4 servings.

Baked Acorn Squash with Rosemary

I discovered this easy way of getting the flavor of herbs into the squash one day while making dinner. You can use the squash to make soup as well as serving it as a vegetable.

1	acorn squash 1	
4	3-inch (7.5 cm) sprigs fresh rosemary 4 (or 6 large sage leaves)	
4 tsp	butter 20 mL	
2 tbsp	brown sugar 30 mL	

1. Cut squash in half lengthwise; with a spoon, scoop out the seeds.
2. Place half of the herbs into the hollow of each squash half. Carefully place the squash halves, cut side down, on a foil-lined baking sheet so the herbs stay enclosed under the squash.
3. Bake in a 400°F (200°C) oven for 40 to 50 minutes, or until very tender when pierced with the tip of a sharp knife.
4. Turn squash halves over; remove and discard herbs. Add butter and brown sugar to hollow and return to oven, cut side up, for 3 to 5 minutes or until butter and sugar begin to bubble.

Makes 2 to 4 servings.

Note
Acorn squash is dark green in color with orange touches, light speckles and ridges running down the length.

Braised Greens

These hearty, leafy veggies are a storehouse of nutritional goodness. In this recipe, use any greens, such as collard, beet, mustard, dandelion or turnip greens, or spinach.

1 tbsp	olive oil	15 mL
1	large onion, chopped	1
1	clove garlic, minced	1
10 cups	chopped kale (discard stems)	2.5 L
8 cups	chopped red or green Swiss chard (including stems)	2 L
1/2 cup	chopped fresh cilantro or basil	125 mL
4 tbsp	red wine vinegar	60 mL
2 tbsp	water	30 mL
2 tsp	granulated sugar	10 mL
2 tbsp	toasted pine nuts	30 mL
	Salt and pepper, to taste	

1. In a Dutch oven or large, heavy saucepan over medium heat, heat oil. Add onion and cook for 7 minutes or until softened.
2. Stir in garlic and greens. Cook, stirring frequently, for about 5 minutes or until greens begin to wilt. Stir in cilantro.
3. Stir together vinegar, water and sugar; stir into greens and cook until greens are tender. Stir in pine nuts and season with salt and pepper.

Makes 4 to 6 servings.

Variations
- Cook bacon or pancetta briefly, then add onions.
- Use red or Vidalia onions.
- Use herb vinegars or lemon juice instead of red wine vinegar.
- Use other fresh herbs, such as oregano or thyme.
- Add minced chili peppers, cayenne pepper or Tabasco.
- Use toasted pecans, walnuts or sesame seeds instead of pine nuts.
- Add a touch of sesame oil or herb oil.
- Add crumbled feta or blue cheese; raisins, dried cranberries or dried cherries.

Broad Beans with Savory and Prosciutto

This is a hearty legume dish that can be eaten on its own as a meal. (Sometimes I eat it for lunch.)

1/3 cup	olive oil	75 mL
1	can (19 oz/540 mL) broad beans, rinsed and well drained	1
2	cloves garlic, minced	2
2 oz	prosciutto, cut into 1/2-inch dice	60 g
1 tbsp	finely chopped fresh savory or sage	15 mL
1 tbsp	dry sherry	15 mL
1 tbsp	finely chopped parsley	15 mL

1. In a large skillet over medium heat, heat oil. Stir in beans; cook for 3 minutes, stirring occasionally.
2. Stir in garlic, prosciutto and savory; cook for 3 minutes, stirring often.
3. Stir in sherry; cook for 1 minute.
4. Stir in parsley. Serve warm.

Makes 2 to 4 servings.

Note

Olive oil is rich in mono-unsaturated fat. Olive oils from different countries and regions have varying tastes much like wines do.

Broiled Tomatoes with Basil Pesto

Serve these delicious tomatoes with eggs for breakfast.

4	large tomatoes 4
4 tbsp	Basil Pesto (see page 141) 60 mL
1 tbsp	grated Parmesan cheese 15 mL

1. Cut tomatoes in half horizontally. Place on baking sheet, cut side up.
2. Spread about 1 tbsp (15 mL) of the pesto over each tomato half. Sprinkle with Parmesan cheese.
3. Broil for 3 to 4 minutes or until bubbly and lightly browned.

Makes 4 servings.

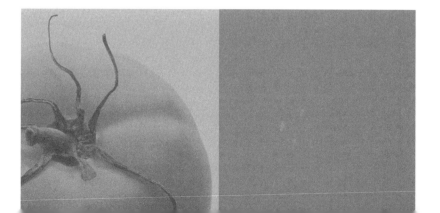

Chick-peas and Tomatoes

If your impression of Indian food is some type of curry, you are in for a pleasant surprise. Chick-peas are a hearty legume, rich in flavor and fiber. Serve with chicken, basmati rice and Raita (see page 142).

3 tbsp	oil 45 mL
2	onions, finely chopped 2
1 tsp	grated fresh ginger 5 mL
1	clove garlic, crushed 1
1/2 tsp	ground turmeric 2 mL
1/4 tsp	crushed hot red pepper flakes, or to taste 1 mL
1	can (28 oz/796 mL) tomatoes 1
1 tbsp	ground coriander (see note below) 15 mL
1	can (19 oz/540 mL) chick-peas, drained and rinsed 1
2 tsp	garam masala (see note below) 10 mL
2 tbsp	lemon juice 30 mL
3 tbsp	chopped fresh cilantro 45 mL
	Cilantro leaves for garnish, optional

1. In a large skillet over medium-high heat, heat oil. Add onions, ginger, garlic, turmeric and hot red pepper flakes; cook for about 7 minutes, or until onions are golden and softened.
2. Drain tomatoes, reserving 1 cup (250 mL) of the juice; chop tomatoes. Add tomatoes and reserved juice, ground coriander and chick-peas; cook, uncovered, for 20 minutes or until thickened.
3. Stir in garam masala and lemon juice; cook for 2 or 3 minutes. Stir in cilantro.
4. Garnish with additional cilantro leaves, if desired.

Makes 4 to 6 servings.

Note
• Ground coriander is the ground seed of the coriander plant. Its fresh leaves are commonly called cilantro.
• Garam masala, which means "hot mixture," is a ground spice blend used in Indian cooking. It can be purchased from Indian stores, comes in many variations and includes such ground spices as cardamom, cinnamon, cloves, coriander, cumin, nutmeg, dried chilies and black pepper.

Grilled Vegetables with Pesto Dressing

Try this tasty vegetable dish at your next outdoor cook-out. Serve with grilled chicken.

2	Japanese eggplants	2
2	medium zucchini	2
2	large portobello mushrooms	2
1	each: sweet red and yellow pepper	1
1	medium red onion	1
1 tbsp	olive oil	15 mL
	Pesto Dressing (recipe follows)	
	Fresh basil sprigs, for garnish	

1. Slice each eggplant into 4 lengthwise slices; slice zucchini into 1/2-inch (1 cm) rounds; leave mushrooms whole or cut in half if very large. Slice peppers into 1-inch (2.5 cm) strips; cut onion into 6 wedges. Toss all vegetables with olive oil.
2. Grill or broil vegetables until tender-crisp and lightly browned.
3. Toss with Pesto Dressing; garnish with basil sprigs.

Makes 4 servings.

Pesto Dressing

1/4 cup	olive oil	60 mL
2 tbsp	Basil Pesto (see page 141)	30 mL
1 tbsp	red wine vinegar or balsamic vinegar	15 mL
2 tsp	lemon juice	10 mL
1	clove garlic, minced	1
	Pepper, to taste	

1. Mix together all ingredients. (Dressing may be made ahead and stored in the refrigerator.)

Herb and Roasted Garlic Mashed Potatoes

These fluffy mashed potatoes will jazz up a "meat and potatoes" meal! Serve with roast chicken, pork chops, grilled steaks, lamb, etc.

3 lb	russet or Yukon Gold potatoes (about 6) 1.5 kg
1/2 cup	18% cream or milk 125 mL
1	whole head roasted garlic (see page 119) 1
3 tbsp	chopped fresh parsley 45 mL
2 tbsp	each: finely chopped fresh basil and chives 30 mL
2 tsp	finely chopped fresh tarragon 10 mL
2 tbsp	butter, optional 30 mL

1. Peel potatoes; boil in salted water until very soft. Drain well.
2. Mash potatoes, keeping hot.
3. In microwave or in a small saucepan over medium heat, heat cream until hot but not boiling. Stir into potatoes. Squeeze roasted garlic from cloves and stir into potatoes.
4. Stir in parsley, basil, chives, tarragon and butter, if using.

Makes 6 servings.

Variation
Omit garlic; replace onion chives with garlic chives.

Minted Peas and Pearl Onions

This classic combination has been updated with the addition of pearl onions and a touch of orange. If you grow your own herbs, grow some orange mint to use in this recipe (omit orange rind). This dish is wonderful with almost any meat but especially lamb, grilled steaks and poultry.

24 (approx.)	pearl onions 24
2 cups	fresh shelled peas 500 mL
1 tbsp	butter 15 mL
1 tsp	grated orange rind 5 mL
2 tbsp	thinly sliced fresh mint leaves 30 mL
	Mint sprig, for garnish

1. Cut a small X in the root end of each unpeeled onion. In a small saucepan, boil onions for about 8 minutes or until tender; drain and rinse under cold water. Skins will slip off easily; drain onions on paper towel.

2. Cook peas just until tender; drain well.

3. In a large skillet over medium-high heat, melt butter. Add onions and cook, stirring, until golden brown.

4. Stir in peas and orange rind. Cook, stirring, just until peas are heated through.

5. Remove from heat; stir in mint leaves and serve. Garnish with sprig of mint.

Makes 4 servings.

New Potatoes with Rosemary and Thyme

The skin of new potatoes is tender and delicious, even more so when cooked with robust Mediterranean herbs and garlic. They are a delightful accompaniment to lamb, poultry or pork.

2 tbsp	olive oil 30 mL
1-1/2 lb	small new potatoes unpeeled, halved 750 g
1	medium onion, chopped 1
2	cloves garlic, minced 2
1 tbsp	chopped fresh rosemary 15 mL
1 tbsp	chopped fresh thyme 15 mL
	Salt and pepper

1. In a large skillet over medium-high heat, heat oil. Add potatoes and onions; cook, stirring frequently, until potatoes are almost soft.
2. Stir in garlic, rosemary and thyme; season with a little salt and pepper. Cook until potatoes are tender and onions are golden.

Makes 4 servings.

tip

This dish can be made with left-over potatoes or, to save time, pre-cook the potatoes, let cool and halve.

Variation

Use 2 tsp (10 mL) Herbes de Provence (see page 3) in place of fresh herbs.

Pesto Potatoes

Add some pizzazz to potatoes! This scalloped potato dish uses basil pesto between the layers with a golden cheese crust on top.

6 large potatoes, peeled and thinly sliced 6

3/4 cup Basil Pesto (see page 141) 175 mL

2/3 cup grated Parmesan cheese 150 mL

1. Cook potato slices in boiling salted water for 3 to 4 minutes until tender but firm; drain well. Let cool slightly. Dry with paper towel to remove excess water.

2. Spread about one-third of the Basil Pesto into the bottom of a 12-cup (3 L) baking dish. Make the next layer using about one-third of the potatoes; spread with another one-third of the remaining pesto and sprinkle with about one-third of the Parmesan. Repeat layers, reserving last one-third of cheese.

3. Cover and bake in a 350°F (180°C) oven for 35 minutes. Remove cover; sprinkle with reserved cheese. Cook uncovered for 5 minutes more, or until potatoes are tender and cheese is golden.

Makes 6 servings.

Puréed Parsnips and Carrots

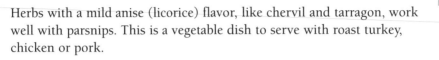

Herbs with a mild anise (licorice) flavor, like chervil and tarragon, work well with parsnips. This is a vegetable dish to serve with roast turkey, chicken or pork.

3 cups	each: chopped carrots and parsnips 750 mL
2 tbsp	butter 30 mL
1 tbsp	finely chopped fresh chervil or tarragon 15 mL
1 tbsp	finely chopped fresh chives 15 mL

1. In a large saucepan, mix together carrots and parsnips. Add water to cover; bring to a boil over high heat. Reduce heat, partially cover and cook for 10 to 12 minutes or until tender.
2. Drain; mash until smooth. Stir in butter, chervil and chives.

Makes 4 servings.

Ratatouille

This dish originates in Provence, France, and is a kind of vegetable stew. It tastes best served the day after you make it.

2	7-inch (18 cm) zucchini 2
1	each: medium green and sweet red pepper 1
1	medium eggplant (about 3/4 lb/375 g), peeled if desired 1
1/4 cup	olive oil 60 mL
2	medium onions, coarsely chopped 2
3	large cloves garlic, minced 3
1	can (28 oz/796 mL) diced tomatoes, with juice 1 (or 4 large tomatoes, seeded and chopped)
1/4 cup	tomato paste 60 mL
2 tsp	chopped fresh thyme 10 mL
1	bay leaf, fresh or dried 1
1/2 cup	chopped fresh basil 125 mL
1/4 cup	chopped fresh parsley 60 mL
	Salt and pepper, to taste

1. Cut zucchini, green and red peppers and eggplant into 1-inch (2.5 cm) chunks; set aside.
2. In a Dutch oven over medium heat, heat oil. Add onions and garlic; cook, stirring, for 5 minutes.
3. Add zucchini, green and red peppers and eggplant; cook, stirring, for about 5 minutes or until almost tender.
4. Stir in tomatoes and juice, tomato paste, thyme and bay leaf. Cook, uncovered, stirring often, for 20 to 30 minutes or until vegetables are tender and sauce is thickened.
5. Stir in basil and parsley; season with salt and pepper.

Makes 4 to 6 servings.

Variations

Ratatouille au Gratin: Spoon prepared ratatouille into shallow individual baking dishes. Sprinkle each with about 1 tbsp (15 mL) Parmesan cheese. Bake in a 375°F (190°C) oven for about 10 minutes or until heated through.

Potato Ratatouille: Use 3 medium potatoes, peeled and chopped, instead of eggplant.

Roasted Sweet Potatoes

Sweet potatoes are rich in Vitamin A. Roasting enhances their natural sweetness. My friend Diane Shearman adds a drizzle of balsamic vinegar to finish them.

2 lb	sweet potatoes, peeled and cut into 1-1/2-inch (3.5 cm) chunks 1 kg
2	medium red onions, cut into wedges 2
3 tbsp	olive oil 45 mL
1 tbsp	minced garlic 15 mL
1 tbsp	finely chopped fresh thyme, rosemary or sage 15 mL
	Salt and pepper, to taste
1 tbsp	balsamic vinegar, optional 15 mL

1. In a large bowl, mix together sweet potatoes, onions, oil, garlic and thyme; toss to coat well.
2. Spread mixture on a baking sheet. Roast in a 425°F (220°C) oven for 40 to 45 minutes; stir twice during baking. Roast until softened and slightly browned.
3. Remove to serving bowl; season with a little salt and pepper. Drizzle with balsamic vinegar (if using).

Makes 4 servings.

Sautéed Portobellos with Rosemary and Thyme

These meaty mushrooms go great with grilled steaks, to top a burger or with scrambled eggs.

2 tbsp	olive oil 30 mL
1 tbsp	butter 15 mL
1/2 lb	portobello mushrooms, sliced or chopped (about 3 large) 250 g
1	clove garlic, minced 1
2 tsp	each: finely chopped fresh rosemary, thyme (or lemon thyme) and parsley 10 mL
1 tbsp	dry sherry or balsamic vinegar, optional 15 mL

1. In a large non-stick skillet over medium-high heat, heat oil and butter until butter foams. Stir in mushrooms, garlic, rosemary, thyme and parsley. Cook, stirring often, for 3 to 5 minutes, or until mushrooms are lightly browned and tender.
2. Stir in sherry (if using).

Makes 4 servings.

Spinach Pie

This quiche-like pie is a great way to enjoy the great taste of spinach. Popeye never had it so good!

8 cups	packed spinach leaves 2 L (or 1 pkg 10 oz/284 g frozen, thawed)
1 tbsp	olive oil or butter 15 mL
2/3 cup	diced shallots or onions 150 mL
3	eggs 3
1-1/2 cups	18% cream 375 mL
1 cup	shredded Gruyère cheese 250 mL
2 tbsp	grated Parmesan cheese 30 mL
2 tbsp	each: finely chopped parsley and chives 30 mL
1 tbsp	finely chopped fresh marjoram 15 mL
	Salt and pepper
1	9-inch (23 cm) pie shell, unbaked 1

1. Cook spinach until wilted; drain very well, squeezing to remove excess water.
2. In a large skillet over medium-low heat, heat oil. Add shallots; cook for about 5 minutes, until softened.
3. In a large bowl, whisk together eggs and cream. Stir in Gruyère, Parmesan, parsley, chives, marjoram, spinach and shallots. Season with a little salt and pepper. Pour spinach mixture into unbaked pie shell.
4. Bake in a 400°F (200°C) oven, on lower rack, for 15 minutes. Reduce heat to 325°F (160°C) and bake for 15 minutes longer, or until knife inserted in center comes out clean.

Makes one 9-inch (23 cm) pie.

tip

Commercially made frozen pie shells are usually smaller; therefore fill only to edge of crust. Remainder of filling may be baked in a well-greased custard cup.

Variations

- Substitute 2 tbsp (30 mL) dill or basil for the marjoram.
- **Broccoli and Cheddar Pie:** Substitute 1 cup (250 mL) chopped cooked broccoli for the spinach, use old Cheddar in place of Gruyère cheese and omit Parmesan.

Vegetable Tempura

This recipe was contributed by my mom, Beti, who has made this dish for many years. She tried it using fresh herbs and was delighted with the result. The herbs become crispy and the flavor mellows.

1	egg, separated 1
1 cup	chicken or vegetable stock 250 mL
2 tsp	oil 10 mL
1 cup	all-purpose flour 250 mL
1 tbsp	cornstarch 15 mL
1 tbsp	grated Parmesan cheese 15 mL
1/2 tsp	salt 5 mL
pinch	garlic powder pinch
2 tbsp	finely chopped fresh parsley or cilantro 30 mL
	Oil for deep frying
4 cups (approx.)	vegetables, cut into 1/4-inch (5 mm) thick pieces or slices: sweet peppers, mushrooms, onion rings, broccoli, cauliflower, thin green beans; fresh herbs, such as curly parsley sprigs, large sage leaves 1 L

1. In a large bowl, whisk together egg yolk, stock and oil.
2. In a small bowl, mix together flour, cornstarch, Parmesan, salt and garlic powder. Whisk into egg mixture until smooth.
3. In a small bowl, using electric mixer, beat egg white until stiff; fold into batter. Fold in parsley.
4. Pour oil into a deep fryer or deep skillet to 1 inch (2.5 cm) deep. Heat to 360°F (185°C).
5. Pat vegetables and herbs dry with paper towel, if necessary. Dip in batter one at a time, allowing batter to drip off. Using tongs, place in hot oil 6 pieces at a time. (If oil is hot enough, they will begin to sizzle immediately.) Deep fry until golden, for about 2 or 3 minutes.
6. Drain on paper towels; keep hot in a 200°F (100°C) oven if desired, until all are cooked.

Makes about 4 servings.

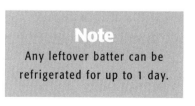

Note
Any leftover batter can be refrigerated for up to 1 day.

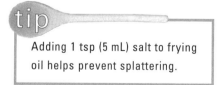

tip

Adding 1 tsp (5 mL) salt to frying oil helps prevent splattering.

Zucchini with Tomatoes and Marjoram

Harvest some of your zucchini while they are still small and pair them with tomatoes and garlic. The crowning touch is the addition of marjoram, sweet cousin to the more earthy oregano. It is a perfect side dish for hot Italian sausages, poultry, lamb, pork or fish.

1 tbsp	olive oil	15 mL
2 lb	small zucchini (about 4)	1 kg
2	medium tomatoes, chopped	2
1	large clove garlic, minced	1
1 tbsp	chopped fresh marjoram or oregano	15 mL
	Salt and pepper, to taste	
2 tbsp	grated Parmesan cheese	30 mL

1. In a large skillet over medium-high heat, heat oil. Add zucchini and cook, stirring frequently, until almost tender.
2. Stir in tomatoes and garlic; cook until zucchini is tender and most of the liquid from the tomatoes has evaporated.
3. Stir in marjoram; season with salt and pepper. Serve with Parmesan sprinkled over top.

Makes 4 servings.

Variation
Omit garlic and add 1 tbsp (15 mL) snipped garlic chives with the marjoram.

Fill your home with the tantalizing aroma of baking. Serve hot biscuits and breads with soups, chili and stews.

BREADS AND BISCUITS

Recipes

Citrus and Sage Scones

These are drop scones, so no rolling or cutting is needed. They are slightly sweet, but the sugar may be omitted for a savory scone to serve with soups. The citrus rind accents the sage nicely.

2 cups	all-purpose flour 500 mL
2 tbsp	granulated sugar 30 mL
2 tsp	baking powder 10 mL
1/2 tsp	salt 2 mL
1/4 cup	butter, slightly softened 60 mL
2 tbsp	finely chopped fresh sage 30 mL
	Finely grated rind of 1 lemon
	Finely grated rind of 1 orange
1/2 cup	milk 125 mL
2	eggs 2

1. In a medium bowl, mix together flour, sugar, baking powder and salt. Cut in butter until mixture resembles coarse crumbs.
2. Using a fork, stir in sage, lemon rind and orange rind.
3. In a small bowl, whisk together milk and eggs; using a fork, quickly stir liquid ingredients into flour mixture just until blended.
4. Using two large spoons, drop dough onto a lightly greased baking sheet, about 2 inches (5 cm) apart. Press lightly to smooth top and slightly flatten.
5. Bake in a 425°F (220°C) oven for 10 to 12 minutes or until golden brown. Serve warm or at room temperature.

Makes 8 to 10.

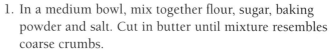

Variations

Lemon Thyme Scones: Omit sugar, lemon and orange rind and sage. Add 1 tbsp (15 mL) finely chopped lemon thyme leaves to replace sage.

Orange-Rosemary Scones: Omit lemon rind and sage. Add 1 tbsp (15 mL) finely chopped rosemary to replace sage.

Savory Scones: Omit sugar; use savory instead of sage.

Cheddar Chive Biscuits

These fluffy biscuits are excellent served hot with soup—try the dill variation with chicken soup. These biscuits also freeze well.

2 cups	all-purpose flour	500 mL
1 tbsp	baking powder	15 mL
1/2 tsp	salt	2 mL
1/4 cup	butter, slightly softened	60 mL
3/4 cup	finely shredded medium or old Cheddar cheese	175 mL
1/4 cup	chopped fresh chives	60 mL
1 cup	milk	250 mL
1 tbsp	melted butter	15 mL

1. In a medium bowl, mix together flour, baking powder and salt. Cut in butter until mixture resembles coarse crumbs.
2. Stir in cheese and chives. Using a fork, quickly stir in milk until mixture forms a soft dough.
3. Turn dough out onto a lightly floured surface; knead 8 to 10 times. Flatten dough to 1/2-inch (1 cm) thickness; cut out with a 2-1/2-inch (6 cm) biscuit cutter. Place on an ungreased cookie sheet; brush tops with melted butter.
4. Bake in a 425°F (220°C) oven for 12 to 15 minutes or until golden brown.

Makes about 1 dozen.

Variations

Dill and Cheddar Biscuits: Use 2 tbsp/30 mL chopped fresh dill in place of chives.

Savory Biscuits: Omit cheese and use 1 tbsp (15 mL) chopped fresh savory in place of chives.

Cheddar Sage Cornbread

This colorful "confetti" cornbread is moist and delicious. Serve with soups or roasted chicken.

1 cup	cornmeal 250 mL
1 cup	all-purpose flour 250 mL
1 tbsp	granulated sugar 15 mL
1 tbsp	baking powder 15 mL
3/4 tsp	salt 4 mL
1/2 tsp	baking soda 2 mL
1-1/2 cups	fresh corn kernels 375 mL (or 12 oz/341 mL can, drained)
1-1/2 cups	shredded old Cheddar cheese 375 mL
1/3 cup	finely chopped sweet red pepper 75 mL
2 tbsp	minced jalapeño pepper, optional 30 mL
2	eggs 2
1 cup	buttermilk (or half plain yogurt and half milk) 250 mL
1/4 cup	vegetable oil 60 mL
3 tbsp	chopped fresh chives 45 mL
2 tbsp	finely chopped fresh sage 30 mL

1. In a large bowl, combine cornmeal, flour, sugar, baking powder, salt and baking soda.
2. Stir in corn, 1-1/4 cup (325 mL) of the cheese, red peppers and jalapeño peppers (if using).
3. In a small bowl, beat eggs with buttermilk and oil; stir into corn mixture just until combined.
4. Spread batter in a greased 9-inch (23 cm) square baking pan or 12 muffin cups. Sprinkle top with remaining 1/4 cup (60 mL) of the cheese. Bake in 400°F (200°C) oven for 25 to 30 minutes (for muffins, bake for 15 to 18 minutes), or until light golden brown and a tester inserted in the center comes out clean.

Makes about 12 servings or 12 muffins.

Variations

Cilantro Cornbread: Use 3 tbsp (45 mL) chopped fresh cilantro in place of sage. Use Monterey Jack cheese in place of Cheddar.

Sun-Dried Tomato Basil or Marjoram Cornbread: Use finely chopped sun-dried tomatoes in place of sweet red pepper; use fresh basil or marjoram in place of sage; omit chives. Use mozzarella or fontina cheese in place of Cheddar. Add 1 tbsp (15 mL) Parmesan cheese sprinkled over cheese on top.

Herbed Bread Sticks

Serve these aromatic bread sticks with a hot bowl of soup, chicken dishes or spaghetti.

2/3 cup	water 150 mL
2 cups	all-purpose or bread flour 500 mL
3 tbsp	each: finely chopped fresh rosemary, sage and thyme 45 mL
1-1/2 tsp	bread machine yeast 7 mL
1 tsp	granulated sugar 5 mL
3/4 tsp	salt 4 mL
1 tbsp	olive or vegetable oil 15 mL
1 tbsp	coarse salt 15 mL

1. In a bread machine, place water, flour, 2 tbsp (30 mL) each of the rosemary, sage and thyme, the yeast, sugar and 3/4 tsp (4 mL) salt, in the order suggested by the manufacturer. Process on the dough/manual cycle. When cycle is complete, remove dough to a lightly floured surface. Cover; let rest for 5 to 10 minutes.

2. Divide dough into 10 equal pieces. Roll each piece on lightly floured surface into a 10-inch (25 cm) rope.

3. Place on a greased baking sheet; brush with oil. Sprinkle with coarse salt and remaining 1 tbsp (15 mL) of the rosemary, sage and thyme. Cover with greased waxed paper; let rise in a warm place for 20 to 30 minutes or until doubled in bulk.

4. Bake in a 425°F (220°C) oven for about 15 minutes or until golden. Remove from baking sheet; let cool on a wire rack.

Makes 10 bread sticks.

Note

This bread may also be made with any traditional white bread dough recipe.

Rosemary and Thyme Focaccia

If you have a bread machine, use it to make your dough! (see recipe next page) Rosemary and thyme are a great combination for this flatbread, which is great served with chicken. If you like, use a head of roasted garlic (see page 119) in place of fresh garlic.

1/3 cup	olive oil 75 mL
1	clove garlic, crushed 1
1 lb	pizza dough or bread dough 500 g
1 tbsp	chopped fresh rosemary 15 mL
1 tbsp	chopped fresh thyme 15 mL
1/2 tsp	coarse salt 2 mL

1. In a small bowl, mix together oil and garlic. Let stand for 1 hour.
2. On a lightly floured surface, knead dough for a couple of minutes. Brush baking sheet with some of the garlic-oil mixture. Transfer dough to the baking sheet and press out into a 10- × 14-inch (25 × 35 cm) oval or rectangle. Cover loosely with plastic wrap and let rise in a warm place for 20 to 30 minutes.
3. With your fingertips, make indentations in the dough. Mix rosemary and thyme into remaining garlic-oil mixture; brush dough with herb-oil mixture. Sprinkle with salt.
4. Bake in a 400°F (200°C) oven for 20 to 25 minutes or until golden. Remove from the pan and let cool slightly on a wire rack. Cut into squares or wedges; serve warm.

Makes 4 to 6 servings.

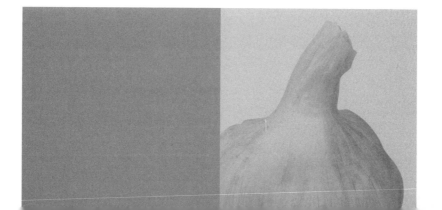

Sage and Red Onion Focaccia

Sage and onions are ideal partners for this savory bread. Serve cut into wedges with soups or stews, or to liven up a meat-and-potatoes dinner. Sweet white onions can be used in place of red onions. If you do not have a bread machine, use 1 lb (500 g) pizza dough.

3 tbsp	olive or vegetable oil	45 mL
3 cups	halved and thinly sliced red onions	750 mL
12	fresh sage leaves	12
1 cup	water	250 mL
3 cups	all-purpose flour	750 mL
3 tbsp	butter	45 mL
2 tbsp	skim milk powder	30 mL
1 tbsp	granulated sugar	15 mL
2 tsp	bread machine yeast	10 mL
1 tsp	salt	5 mL
1 tbsp	cornmeal	15 mL

1. In a large skillet over medium heat, heat oil. Add onions; reduce heat to medium-low. Cook for 20 to 30 minutes, stirring occasionally, until onions are softened and golden. Stir in sage leaves; cook for 1 minute. Let cool.

2. In bread machine, place water, flour, butter, milk powder, sugar, yeast and salt, in the order suggested by manufacturer. Process on the dough/manual cycle. When the cycle is complete, remove dough to a lightly floured surface. Cover; let rest for 5 to 10 minutes.

3. Roll out dough into a 10- × 14-inch (25 × 35 cm) rectangle. Sprinkle cornmeal onto a baking sheet; place dough on top. Cover; let rise in warm place for 20 to 30 minutes or until doubled in bulk.

4. With your fingertips, make indentations all over the dough. Spread onion and sage mixture over dough.

5. Bake in a 400°F (200°C) oven for 20 to 25 minutes or until golden. Remove from the pan and let cool slightly on a wire rack. Cut into squares and wedges; serve warm.

Makes 4 to 6 servings.

Make the grande finale to your meal a dessert kissed with fresh herbs and decorated with edible flowers. Infuse the cream or milk you use to make cakes or puddings with fresh herbs. Use herb butters to make crusts for tarts or pies; use herb syrups to glaze a loaf or muffins. Herb sugars add sparkle to the top of cookies or over fruit. The herbs most commonly used with desserts are cinnamon basil, lavender, lemon herbs (lemon balm, lemon basil, lemon thyme, lemon verbena, etc.), mints and rosemary.

DESSERTS

Recipes

Chocolate Mint Fondue

Serve with slices of fresh pineapple, small strawberries, cubes of angel food cake, etc. Recipe may be doubled.

1/2 cup	whipping cream 125 mL
1/2 cup	chopped fresh mint (spearmint, orange mint or chocolate mint) 125 mL
6 oz	bittersweet chocolate 175 g

1. In a small saucepan, combine cream, mint and chocolate. Heat just to boiling point; remove from heat. Let stand for 20 minutes.

2. Strain through a sieve; discard mint. When ready to serve, transfer to a fondue pot and warm slowly.

Makes 4 to 6 servings.

Chocolate Mint Sauce

This is a great sauce to pour over ice cream or pears.

8 oz	semi-sweet chocolate	250 g
3/4 cup	chopped fresh mint	175 mL
1/2 cup	granulated sugar	125 mL
1/2 cup	water	125 mL
2 tbsp	butter	30 mL

1. In a medium saucepan, mix together chocolate, mint, sugar and water. Over medium heat, bring to a boil; boil gently for 3 minutes, stirring constantly.
2. Remove from heat; whisk in butter. Let stand for 20 minutes. Strain through a sieve; discard mint.
3. May be served warm or cold. Store in a covered jar in the refrigerator; reheat in a saucepan over low heat or microwave, stirring occasionally.

Makes about 1 cup (250 mL).

Variation
Lavender-Chocolate Sauce: Use 2 tbsp (30 mL) fresh lavender flowers instead of mint.

Cream Puffs with Chocolate-Mint Cream

These small cream puffs are just the thing for an elegant dessert. If you like, serve them with raspberries or sliced strawberries. The Chocolate-Mint Cream can also be used for a chocolate cake or a jelly roll.

Cream Puffs

1/2 cup	water	125 mL
1/4 cup	butter	60 mL
1/2 cup	all-purpose flour	125 mL
2	eggs	2

Chocolate-Mint Cream (recipe follows)

Icing sugar and mint leaves, for garnish

1. In a medium saucepan over high heat, bring water and butter to a boil.
2. Stir in flour all at once; beat until mixture forms a ball that comes away from the sides of the pan. Remove from heat; let cool for 5 minutes.
3. Using an electric mixer, beat in eggs one at a time, beating until smooth after each addition. Transfer to a bowl; refrigerate for 10 minutes.
4. Drop dough by spoonfuls onto a lightly greased or parchment-lined baking sheet, to make 10 cream puffs, mounding puffs high in center.
5. Bake in a 450°F (220°C) oven for 10 minutes. Reduce temperature to 300°F (150°C); bake for 15 to 20 minutes, or until they are golden brown and appear dry. Remove from the oven; cut a small slit in each puff to release steam. Turn the oven off; return puffs to the oven for 30 minutes, leaving oven door ajar.
6. Cut a small piece off the top of each puff; remove dough filaments from inside. Replace tops. Let cool completely.
7. Spoon about 1/4 cup (60 mL) Chocolate-Mint Cream into each cream puff; replace tops. Dust with icing sugar. Garnish plate with mint leaves.

Makes 10 puffs.

Chocolate-Mint Cream

1 cup	whipping cream	250 mL
1/4 cup	chopped mint leaves (spearmint or peppermint)	60 mL
2 oz	semi-sweet chocolate	60 g

1. In a small saucepan over medium-low heat, mix together cream, mint and chocolate. Heat, stirring often, until chocolate melts. Stir until smooth.
2. Refrigerate until well chilled. Strain through a sieve; discard mint.
3. Using an electric mixer, beat chocolate mixture until peaks form.

Makes 1-1/2 cups (375 mL).

Lavender Ice Cream

Several years ago while visiting my brother Richard in London, England, I thought we would try making lavender ice cream in his new ice cream maker. So we set off to find some lavender. Unfortunately it was the end of the summer and most of the lavender was past blooming. Luckily we were able to pinch a few last flower heads from some front gardens in the neighborhood; we made this delicious ice cream, which we enjoyed with fresh sliced peaches. It would also be very good with raspberries, sliced strawberries or nectarines.

4	egg yolks	4
3/4 cup	granulated sugar	175 mL
3/4 cup	half-and-half cream (18%)	175 mL
2 tbsp	fresh lavender florets (or 2 tsp/10 mL dried)	30 mL
3/4 cup	whipping cream (35%)	175 mL

1. In a medium bowl, whisk together egg yolks and sugar until light in color and foamy.
2. In a medium saucepan, combine half-and-half cream and lavender florets. Over medium heat, bring to a boil; simmer for 1 minute. Remove from heat and strain through a sieve; discard lavender.
3. Slowly whisk infused cream into egg yolk mixture. Return to saucepan and cook over low heat, stirring constantly, until the mixture thickens slightly and coats the back of a spoon. Do not allow to boil. Pour back into bowl and refrigerate until very cold.
4. In a medium bowl, with an electric mixer, beat whipping cream until stiff peaks form. Fold into cold lavender custard. Pour into ice cream maker and process, or pour into a freezer container and freeze.

Makes 4 servings.

Note

Use only organically grown lavender flowers, free from herbicides and pesticides. Remove the tiny florets from the flower heads to use.

Variation

Chocolate-Mint Ice Cream: Use 1/3 cup (75 mL) finely chopped fresh mint in place of lavender. Break 3 oz (90 g) semi-sweet chocolate into pieces; stir into hot cream until melted.

Lavender Peach Galette

This is an easy-to-make free-form pie that looks very rustic. The lavender adds an interesting flavor that enhances the peaches. Serve it with French vanilla ice cream or raspberry frozen yogurt.

8	large peaches (about 2 lb/1 kg), peeled and pitted, cut into 1/4-inch (5 mm) slices 8
2 tbsp	lemon juice 30 mL
1 tbsp	fresh or dried lavender flowers, crushed 15 mL
1/2 cup	granulated sugar 125 mL
2 tbsp	cornstarch 30 mL
1	pastry for double pie crust 1
1/2 cup	ground almonds 125 mL
1	egg yolk 1
1 tsp	water 5 mL
2 tbsp	granulated sugar 30 mL

1. In a large bowl, toss peaches with lemon juice, lavender and 1/4 cup (60 mL) of the sugar. Let stand for about 1 hour; drain peaches, reserving juice. Mix together remaining 1/4 cup (60 mL) of the sugar and cornstarch; stir into peaches.

2. On a lightly floured surface, roll out pastry to 14-inch (35 cm) round. Place on a large baking sheet. Sprinkle ground almonds over pastry to within 2 inches (5 cm) of edge. Drain peaches and arrange on top of almonds. Fold the edges of the pastry in toward the center, overlapping slightly to form a 2-inch (5 cm) border. Combine egg yolk and water; brush over border and sprinkle with sugar. (Put into oven right away to prevent crust from becoming soggy.)

3. Bake in a 425°F (220°C) oven for 15 minutes. Reduce temperature to 375°F (190°C) and bake for 30 to 40 minutes longer, or until peaches are tender and crust is golden brown. (If crust browns too quickly, cover with foil.) Use reserved juice to brush over peaches several times during cooking.

Makes 8 servings.

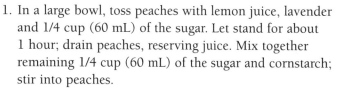

Lavender Lemon Cream in Phyllo Cups

This dessert starts with an easy microwave lemon curd then folds herb-infused whipped cream into it. This light filling is spooned into crispy paper-thin phyllo cups and topped with assorted fresh berries.

2	whole eggs	2
1	egg yolk	1
2/3 cup	granulated sugar	150 mL
1 tbsp	grated lemon rind	15 mL
4 tbsp	lemon juice	60 mL
1 tbsp	butter	15 mL
1/2 cup	whipping cream (35%)	125 mL
1 tsp	dried lavender flowers (or 2 tsp/10 mL fresh)	5 mL
9	Phyllo Cups (recipe follows)	9
1 cup	fresh berries (such as raspberries, blueberries, sliced strawberries)	250 mL
	Small mint sprigs, for garnish	

Variation
Minted Lemon Cream: Use 2 tbsp (30 mL) finely chopped fresh mint in place of lavender.

1. In a large microwavable bowl, whisk together eggs, egg yolk, sugar, lemon rind and juice. Microwave on high for 2 minutes; whisk and microwave for 2 minutes longer. Whisk in butter, about 1 teaspoon (5 mL) at a time. Set aside.

2. In a small saucepan over medium-high heat, heat cream and lavender just to a boil. Remove from heat; let cool. Strain and discard lavender; refrigerate cream for 20 minutes or until very cold. Using an electric mixer, whip cream.

3. Reserve 1/2 cup (125 mL) of the whipped cream; fold remaining whipped cream into the egg mixture.

4. Divide the lemon cream among phyllo cups; top with dollop of the reserved whipped cream, berries and a mint sprig.

Phyllo Cups

Stack 2 sheets of phyllo pastry; brush top lightly with melted butter. Cut in half lengthwise, then in 3 crosswise. Place squares into 6 greased large muffin cups. Repeat with 2 more sheets, placing a second square crosswise over each of the first squares. Repeat with 2 more sheets, this time using the 6 squares to make 3 additional cups. Bake on lower rack of a 375°F (190°C) oven for about 6 minutes, or until golden brown. Remove from pan to baking rack; let cool. Fill just before serving.

Makes 9 servings.

Lavender Shortbread

This lovely shortbread has a subtle hint of lavender and a tender texture.

1 cup	butter, softened	250 mL
1/2 cup	Lavender Sugar (see page 37)	125 mL
1-1/2 cups	all-purpose flour	375 mL
1/2 cup	cornstarch	125 mL
1 tsp	fresh or dried lavender florets, crushed	5 mL
1 tsp	granulated sugar or Lavender Sugar (see Herb Sugars, page 38)	5 mL

1. In a large bowl, using an electric mixer, cream butter until very smooth. Beat in 1/2 cup (125 mL) of Lavender Sugar a little at a time, until light and fluffy.
2. In a small bowl, mix together flour, cornstarch and lavender; stir into butter mixture just until blended.
3. Press into a 9-inch (23 cm) fluted round tart pan with removable base, or a 9-inch (23 cm) square cake pan. Score the top with a knife to create 12 wedges (in a fluted pan) or 27 bars (in a square pan: 3 bars × 9 bars). Prick all over with a fork. Sprinkle top with granulated sugar.
4. Bake on the lower rack of a 300°F (150°C) oven for 25 to 35 minutes or until firm to the touch and golden. Let cool slightly; slice into wedges or bars along scored lines.

Makes 12 wedges or 27 bars.

tip

For a speedy Lavender Sugar, combine 1/2 cup (125 mL) granulated sugar and 2 tbsp (30 mL) fresh lavender florets (or 2 tsp/10 mL dried) in food processor. Process until finely ground. Cream as above with butter, but omit the additional 1 tsp/5 mL lavender flowers.

Lemon Thyme Sugar Cookies

The subtle lemony flavor of lemon thyme elevates the simple sugar cookie to new heights.

1/2 cup	butter, softened	125 mL
3/4 cup	granulated sugar	175 mL
1	egg	1
1/2 tsp	vanilla	2 mL
1-1/2 cups	all-purpose flour	375 mL
1/2 tsp	baking powder	2 mL
1/4 tsp	baking soda	1 mL
1/4 tsp	salt	1 mL
4 tsp	very finely chopped fresh lemon thyme	20 mL
	(or 2 tbsp/30 mL cinnamon basil)	

1. In a large bowl, using an electric mixer, cream together butter and sugar. Beat in egg and vanilla.
2. In a small bowl, mix together flour, baking powder, baking soda and salt. Stir into creamed mixture.
3. Stir in lemon thyme. Divide dough in half; shape into two 7-inch (18 cm) logs. Wrap each in plastic wrap; refrigerate for 1 hour.
4. Cut logs into slices 1/4 inch (5 mm) thick. Place on greased baking sheets; bake in a 350°F (180°C) oven for 10 to 12 minutes or until slightly browned. Let cool on racks; store in a covered container.

Makes 36 to 40.

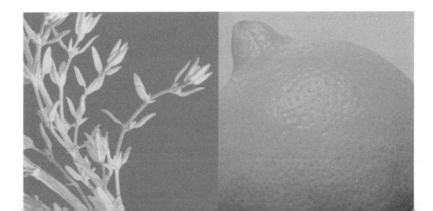

Lemon and Rosemary Cookies

These cookies are made with a bit of cornmeal, which gives them a pleasing crunch.

3/4 cup	butter, softened	175 mL
1 cup	sifted icing sugar	250 mL
1	egg	1
2 tbsp	grated lemon rind	30 mL
1 tbsp	lemon juice	15 mL
3/4 tsp	vanilla	4 mL
1-1/2 cups	all-purpose flour	375 mL
1/4 cup	cornmeal	60 mL
3/4 tsp	baking powder	4 mL
1/4 tsp	each: baking soda and salt	1 mL
2 tsp	finely chopped fresh rosemary	10 mL

1. In a large bowl, using an electric mixer, cream butter and sugar until fluffy; beat in egg. Beat in lemon rind, juice and vanilla.
2. In a separate bowl, mix together flour, cornmeal, baking powder, baking soda, salt and rosemary; stir into creamed mixture. Shape dough into a ball; cover with plastic wrap and refrigerate for 1 hour.
3. Roll dough into small balls, using about 1 tbsp (15 mL) of dough per cookie. Place on a lightly greased baking sheet, leaving about 2 inches (5 cm) between each cookie; flatten with fork.
4. Bake in a 350°F (180°C) oven for 15 to 17 minutes or until light golden brown.

Makes about 40.

Orange and Basil Biscotti

Biscotti (meaning "twice baked") are not as difficult to make as you might think. Many different types can be found in gourmet coffee shops, and I'm sure you'll enjoy this version with basil and orange. Give them as a gift from your kitchen in small cello bags (found in party stores) and tied with a decorative ribbon.

1/2 cup	butter	125 mL
1 cup	granulated sugar	250 mL
1	egg	1
1/4 cup	orange juice	60 mL
	Grated rind from 1 medium orange	
2-1/4 cups	all-purpose flour	560 mL
2 tbsp	cornmeal	30 mL
1 tsp	baking powder	5 mL
1/2 tsp	salt	2 mL
3/4 cup	coarsely chopped pistachios	175 mL
2 tbsp	finely chopped fresh basil or cinnamon basil	30 mL

1. In a large bowl, cream together butter and sugar until fluffy; beat in egg. Beat in orange juice and rind.
2. In a separate bowl, mix together flour, cornmeal, baking powder and salt; add to creamed mixture all at once, stirring just until combined. Stir in pistachios and basil.
3. Divide dough in half. With floured hands, shape each half into a log about 12 inches (30 cm) long by 2 inches (5 cm) wide, leaving top slightly rounded. Place on a lightly greased baking sheet about 4 inches (10 cm) apart.
4. Bake in a 325°F (160°C) oven for 30 minutes or until just beginning to brown. Let cool on the baking sheet for 10 minutes.
5. Using a sharp knife, cut logs into 1/2-inch (1 cm) slices on a slight diagonal. Arrange slices upright on the baking sheet about 1 inch (2.5 cm) apart.
6. Reduce oven temperature to 300°F (150°C); bake for 20 to 25 minutes or until firm and dry. Let cool.
7. Store in an airtight container for up to 1 week.

Makes about 40.

Mint and Lime Sorbet

Sorbets can be served between courses to cleanse the palate or as a light, refreshing dessert.

2 cups	water	500 mL
2/3 cup	granulated sugar	150 mL
1/3 cup	chopped fresh mint	75 mL
1/2 cup	clear or light corn syrup	125 mL
1 tbsp	finely grated lime rind	15 mL
1/3 cup	lime juice	75 mL
2	egg whites	2
	mint sprigs, for garnish	

1. In a small saucepan, combine water, sugar and mint. Bring to a boil over high heat, stirring to dissolve sugar. Remove from heat. Let stand for 30 minutes; strain through a sieve and discard mint, squeezing to extract all of the syrup.

2. Return mint syrup to saucepan. Stir in corn syrup, lime rind and juice. Pour into a 9-inch (23 cm) square metal baking pan (or freezer trays). Freeze until firm.

3. Remove lime ice in chunks to a large bowl. Beat, using an electric mixer, until smooth and thick. (Or pulse in a food processor; transfer to a large bowl.)

4. In a medium bowl, beat egg whites with an electric mixer until stiff peaks form. Fold egg whites into lime mixture; return to pan and freeze again until firm. Let stand at room temperature until softened enough to scoop. Serve garnished with mint sprigs.

Makes 4 to 6 servings.

Variation
Lemon Lavender Sorbet: Use 2 tbsp (30 mL) fresh lavender (or 2 tsp/10 mL dried) in place of mint. Use lemon rind and juice in place of lime.

Note
Sorbet may also be made in an ice cream maker following the manufacturer's directions.

Minted Mango Mousse

This is a refreshing, light dessert. It is especially good to end a spicy, hot meal, such as those of Indian or Thai cuisines.

1	pkg (8 oz/250 g) cream cheese, softened 1
1/3 cup	granulated sugar 75 mL
2 cups	chopped mango 500 mL
1	envelope unflavored gelatin 1
1 tbsp	finely chopped fresh mint 15 mL
	Whipped cream and mint leaves, for garnish

1. In a large bowl, using an electric mixer, beat cream cheese and sugar until smooth.
2. Purée mango in a food processor until smooth. Beat mango into cream cheese mixture until well combined.
3. Prepare gelatin according to package directions. Stir into mango mixture.
4. Fold in mint. Pour into a serving bowl or stemmed glasses; cover with plastic wrap and refrigerate for about 2 hours or until set. Garnish each serving with a dollop of whipped cream and a small mint sprig.

Makes 4 to 6 servings.

Orange Mint Baked Custards

Orange mint has a lovely, subtle flavor that you will have to taste to believe. I have also infused the milk for making tapioca with orange mint.

2 cups	homogenized milk	500 mL
1/2 cup	finely chopped orange mint, lemon balm or cinnamon basil	125 mL
	(or 1 tbsp/15 mL dried lavender)	
4	eggs	4
1/3 cup	granulated sugar	75 mL
pinch	salt	pinch
1/2 tsp	vanilla	2 mL
	Violas or Johnny-jump-ups (see "Edible Flowers," page 38), or sprigs of orange mint or lemon balm, for garnish	

1. In a medium saucepan over medium-high heat, heat milk and mint, stirring occasionally, just until it comes to a boil. Remove from heat; let stand for 20 minutes. Strain; discard mint.

2. In a large bowl, beat together eggs, sugar and salt. Slowly whisk warm milk mixture into eggs. Whisk in vanilla.

3. Place four 3/4-cup (175 mL) ramekins or custard cups in a baking dish; pour egg mixture into ramekins. Pour hot water into baking dish until it comes halfway up the sides of the ramekins.

4. Bake in a 350°F (180°C) oven for 20 to 25 minutes, or until a knife inserted in the center comes out clean. Remove ramekins from water; let cool to room temperature. Cover with plastic wrap; refrigerate until chilled and firm, about 3 hours or overnight. If desired, garnish with edible flowers or mint sprigs.

Makes 4 servings.

Variation

Crème Brûlée Topping: Just before serving, sprinkle each custard with 1/2 tsp (2 mL) granulated sugar. Broil until sugar caramelizes; serve immediately.

Poached Pears with Rosemary

Here's an interesting twist to poached pears, using cranberry juice, rosemary and orange. I like to cook the pears already halved and cored, but they can be poached whole; double the recipe and place in a saucepan just large enough to fit the peeled pears standing upright.

2 cups	cranberry juice 500 mL
1/2 cup	granulated sugar 125 mL
1 tbsp	coarsely grated orange rind 15 mL
1 tbsp	minced fresh rosemary 15 mL
2	large firm, ripe Bartlett or Packham pears 2 (or 4 small)
1 tbsp	orange liqueur or brandy, optional 15 mL
	Whipped cream or vanilla ice cream and small rosemary or mint sprigs, for garnish

Variation
Use 1/4 cup (60 mL) finely chopped orange mint instead of minced fresh rosemary.

1. In a large saucepan, mix together cranberry juice, sugar, orange rind and rosemary.
2. Peel and halve pears; remove cores, stems and blossom ends. Place pears in the saucepan with juice mixture.
3. Over high heat, bring to a boil. Reduce heat; simmer, uncovered, for 15 to 20 minutes or until pears are tender.
4. Using a slotted spoon, remove pears; cover and refrigerate. Increase heat to high; boil juice mixture until reduced to about 1 cup (250 mL). Strain, discarding solids. Stir in liqueur (if using); refrigerate.
5. To serve, place pear halves on 4 individual serving plates; drizzle each with one-quarter of the syrup. Spoon a dollop of whipped cream into the center of each pear half. (Or slice pear halves lengthwise, not slicing all the way through at the stem end; fan out and place on plates with a scoop of ice cream.) Garnish with rosemary or mint sprigs.

Makes 4 servings.

Rosemary and Lemon Custard Cakes

This is a simple but impressive dessert. As it bakes, it separates into a bottom layer of lemon custard with a top layer of soft sponge cake. Rosemary, with its piney essence, combines well with lemon.

2 tbsp	butter 30 mL
3/4 cup	granulated sugar 175 mL
1/4 cup	all-purpose flour 60 mL
pinch	salt pinch
2 tsp	grated lemon rind 10 mL
1/4 cup	lemon juice 60 mL
1/2 tsp	finely chopped fresh rosemary 2 mL
3	eggs, separated 3
1 cup	milk 250 mL
1/4 cup	sifted icing sugar 60 mL
	Icing sugar
	Rosemary sprigs, candied violets or violas, for garnish

1. In a large bowl, cream together butter and sugar. Stir in flour, salt, lemon rind, lemon juice and rosemary.

2. In a medium bowl, using an electric mixer, beat egg yolks until thick; beat in milk. Stir into creamed mixture.

3. In a medium bowl, beat egg whites with 1/4 cup (60 mL) icing sugar until soft peaks form. Fold into creamed mixture.

4. Divide mixture among 6 lightly greased 1-cup (250 mL) ramekins; place ramekins in a large baking pan. Pour enough hot water into pan to come halfway up ramekins.

5. Bake in a 350°F (180°C) oven for 30 to 35 minutes or until tops are puffed and golden brown. (Cake will rise to top and custard will form on bottom.)

6. Dust with icing sugar; garnish with rosemary sprigs and/or candied violets or violas. Serve warm, at room temperature or chilled.

Makes 6 servings.

Strawberry and Melon Salad with Minted Yogurt Dressing

This very light, refreshing summertime salad is perfect to serve as an appetizer or a luncheon main course with grainy bread and cold chicken or fish. The low-fat dressing is slightly sweet, with a hint of lemon and fresh mint.

Salad

1	head Boston lettuce	1
1	honeydew melon, cut into bite-size chunks	1
1	cantaloupe, cut into bite-size chunks or made into small balls using melon baller	1
1 cup	sliced strawberries or whole blueberries	250 mL
	Minted Yogurt Dressing (recipe follows)	

1. Tear lettuce leaves into bite-size pieces; divide among salad plates.
2. Top lettuce with melon and cantaloupe pieces and strawberries.
3. Drizzle with Minted Yogurt Dressing.

Makes 4 to 6 servings.

Minted Yogurt Dressing

1/2 cup	low-fat plain yogurt	125 mL
2 tbsp	liquid honey	30 mL
2 tsp	lemon juice	10 mL
2 tsp	finely chopped mint	10 mL
1 tsp	finely grated lemon rind	5 mL

1. In a small bowl, whisk together yogurt, honey and lemon juice.
2. Stir in mint and lemon rind.

Variation
Use 3 cups (750 mL) sliced strawberries and kiwifruit or 3 cups (750 mL) sliced mango and raspberries in place of melon, cantaloupe and strawberries.

Variation
Use lemon balm in place of mint.

Sweet Herb Crêpes

Serve these crêpes for brunch or to end a meal with a touch of flair. Crêpes can be made ahead, wrapped well and refrigerated for up to two days, or frozen with waxed paper between the layers and placed in a freezer bag. Thaw completely before unwrapping and separating.

4	eggs	4
1/4 cup	granulated sugar	60 mL
pinch	salt	pinch
2 cups	all-purpose flour	500 mL
2 cups	milk	500 mL
1/4 cup	melted butter or oil	60 mL
2 tbsp	finely chopped fresh mint or lemon balm	30 mL
1 tsp	vanilla	5 mL
	or 2 tsp (10 mL) finely grated lemon or orange rind, or 2 tbsp (30 mL) orange liqueur	

tip

Batter should be the consistency of heavy cream. If it is too thick, stir in a bit more milk.

1. In a large bowl, using an electric mixer, beat eggs, sugar and salt.

2. Gradually beat in flour alternately with milk; beat until smooth.

3. Beat in butter, mint and vanilla until smooth. Let stand at room temperature for at least 1 hour. (May be refrigerated overnight.)

4. Heat a non-stick skillet (7-1/2 inches/19 cm measured across base) over medium-high heat. Grease lightly with butter.

5. Stir crêpe batter a few times. For each crêpe, pour about 1/4 cup (60 mL) of the batter into the skillet. Immediately rotate pan to spread batter thinly and evenly. Cook until the underside is golden brown, about 1 minute. (Adjust heat if cooking too quickly or slowly.) Cook until the top feels dry to touch; flip over, if desired, and cook for about 20 seconds. Repeat with remaining batter. Stack crêpes on top of one another.

6. Fold crêpes into quarters; open up one fold to make a "cone" shape and fill with fruit or ice cream. If filling with fruit, stir a little vanilla yogurt or soft cheese product into fruit, if desired.

Crêpe Variations

Chocolate-Mint

Add 1 tbsp (15 mL) finely chopped fresh mint or orange mint and 2 squares of melted semi-sweet chocolate to the crêpe batter. Use for strawberry, banana or mixed berry (strawberries, raspberries and blackberries) crêpes.

Peach Melba

Fill crêpes with vanilla ice cream, sliced peaches and raspberries. Dust with icing sugar; serve with whipped cream or Lavender Whipped Cream (see page 202, step 2).

Tropical Delight

Use cinnamon basil (2 tbsp/30 mL) in the crêpes in place of mint; fill crêpes with a mixture of pineapple, banana and papaya; sprinkle with toasted coconut or toasted sliced almonds.

Strawberry-Kiwi

Fill crêpes with equal amounts of raspberries and chopped kiwis.

Sip a hot lemony tea or a refreshing minty cold beverage to soothe and assuage body and soul. Drink in the sunshine that the herbs basked in while they grew, and enjoy a bit of aromatherapy, too. Herbs add a special touch of interest to popular beverages, whether it is an ice-cold lemonade, a refreshing white wine spritzer or a soothing cup of hot tea.

HERBAL TEAS AND BEVERAGES

Recipes

Herb Teas

These herbs are great for making teas: any lemony herb (such as lemon balm, lemon basil, lemon thyme, lemon verbena), lavender (flowers or leaves), mints, oregano, rosemary and sage. Feel free to combine leaves, like lemon balm and lavender, rosemary and orange mint, mints and any lemon herbs. Or try sage tea with a spoonful of Lemon Verbena Honey (See "Herb Honeys," page 36.)

Any of these herbs (fresh or dried) can be added to a pot of your favorite store-bought black tea or other herb teas as well. Use any of them you wish to make iced tea; chill and sweeten to taste. Add fresh herb leaves to ice in a tall glass to serve.

All of these herbs retain their flavor well when dried. Store in glass jars with lids, away from heat and light. (See "Drying Herbs," page 17.)

Basic Recipe for Herb Tea

Use about 2 cups (500 mL) hot or boiling water and 1 to 2 tbsp (15 to 30 mL) fresh herbs (1 to 2 tsp dried), or to taste.

Tips on Making Herb Teas

- Use only the flowers or leaves; do not use stems.
- Use a pot for making hot tea so you do not lose too much aromatic oil.
- Use hot (boiled) water for fresh herbs and boiling water for dried herbs.
- Allow to herbs infuse/steep for about 5 minutes. Taste to determine if tea is to your liking; you can leave to infuse/steep longer, add more herbs or use less water the next time.
- It is not necessary to remove the leaves. If desired, pour through a small strainer into cups or mugs.
- Use juices to infuse/steep leaves: apple juice or cider, cranberry juice.

Mint Mimosa

This drink, named after a tropical flower, is a champagne and orange juice beverage served at brunch. Serve it well chilled (but without ice) in tall, chilled champagne glasses. If desired, garnish with edible flowers such as begonias (see "Edible Flowers," page 38).

1 cup	frozen orange juice concentrate 250 mL
1/3 cup	chopped fresh mint (such as peppermint, spearmint or orange mint) 75 mL
2	bottles (750 mL) well-chilled champagne 2
	Begonia flowers or mint sprigs, for garnish

1. In blender, purée orange juice and mint. Strain through a sieve, pressing to extract juice; discard mint.
2. Pour about 2 tbsp (30 mL) mint-orange concentrate into a chilled champagne glass. Fill with chilled champagne. Garnish with begonias or mint sprigs. Serve immediately.

Makes 6 to 8 servings.

Herbed Wine

Herbs and wines go well together. Drink herbed wine straight, or use to make spritzers by adding carbonated water or soda water and a slice of lemon or lime.

1	bottle (24 oz/750 mL) wine (see below) 1
1 cup	chopped herbs (see below) 250 mL

1. Pour wine into a large pitcher.
2. Stir in chopped herbs. Stir with wooden spoon to bruise leaves.
3. Cover and refrigerate for about 8 hours. Strain through a sieve; discard leaves. Taste. The herbs should be recognizable but not overpowering; dilute with more wine if too strong.

Variations

Dry White Wine, White Zinfandel or Fruit Wines: Use lemon balm, lemon verbena or mints. If desired, add slices of strawberry or raspberries to fruit wines.

Red Wine: Use lemon balm or 1/4 cup (60 mL) rosemary.

Sangria: Use orange mint or 1/4 cup (60 mL) rosemary.

Fruit Smoothie

Here's a great breakfast or snack drink that whips up in no time in the blender.

1-1/2 cups	plain yogurt 375 mL
3/4 cup	chopped fresh fruit (or whole raspberries or blueberries) 175 mL
2 tbsp	honey or sugar, or to taste 30 mL
1 tbsp	finely chopped fresh mint, lemon balm or lavender flowers 15 mL
	Mint sprigs, for garnish

1. In blender combine all ingredients except mint sprigs. Purée until smooth.
2. Pour into tall glasses; garnish with mint sprigs.

Makes 2 servings.

tip

Use frozen, thawed fruit in place of fresh fruit, or fruit juice concentrates in place of honey. Add to taste.

Variations
- Use 3 tbsp (45 mL) Chocolate Mint Sauce (see page 198) in place of honey; add 1 medium ripe banana.
- Try these fruit combinations: raspberry or strawberry and mango; raspberry or strawberry and kiwi or banana; raspberry and blueberry; blueberry and cantaloupe; orange, papaya and mango or passion fruit; pineapple, papaya and banana.

Lavender Lemonade

Lavender provides a lovely aroma to enjoy as you sip. Make lemonade with fresh lemon juice and sugar syrup, if desired, and use the steeped lavender as part of the water you would use.

1/4 cup	fresh lavender flowers 60 mL (or 2 tbsp/30 mL dried)
1 cup	boiling water 250 mL
1	can (355 mL) frozen lemonade concentrate, thawed 1
	Long stems of lavender, for garnish

1. In a small bowl, place lavender flowers; pour boiling water over top. Stir to submerge all the flowers. Cover with plastic wrap and let stand for about 30 minutes. Strain through a sieve; discard lavender.

2. In a large pitcher, mix lemonade according to package directions, using lavender water as part of the water needed to reconstitute.

3. Pour over ice into tall glasses; garnish each with a long lavender stem. If desired, place several lavender flower heads in the pitcher.

Makes about 6 servings.

Variations

Sparkling Lavender Lemonade: Use only half the water called for on the lemonade package; fill glasses half full with lavender lemonade and top with carbonated mineral water or soda water.

Lavender Cranberry Cocktail: Use frozen cranberry cocktail in place of frozen lemonade.

Rosemary Cranberry Cocktail: Use 2 tbsp (30 mL) chopped rosemary in place of lavender; use frozen cranberry cocktail in place of frozen lemonade.

Lavender Peach Iced Tea: Use frozen peach iced tea in place of frozen lemonade.

Minted Lemonade: Use 1/2 cup (125 mL) chopped fresh mint or lemon balm in place of lavender, but add directly to pitcher. Refrigerate about 4 hours, then strain through a sieve. Add a few fresh mint leaves to the glasses with ice and pour in drink.

Mint Julep

This is a refreshing summer drink originating in the southern United States. It's definitely oozing with southern charm!

10	large fresh mint leaves	10
1 tsp	granulated sugar	5 mL
2 tbsp	boiling water	30 mL
	crushed ice	
2 oz	bourbon	60 mL
	Fresh mint sprigs, for garnish	

1. In a small glass measuring cup, place mint leaves. Sprinkle leaves with sugar; use a spoon to bruise leaves against sugar. Pour in boiling water; stir to dissolve sugar.
2. Pour mint mixture into a tall glass. Fill glass three-quarters full with crushed ice. Pour in bourbon; garnish with fresh mint sprigs.

Makes 1 serving.

Variations

Mocktail: In Step 2, fill glass one-third full with thawed frozen juice concentrate, such as orange, pineapple or peach, or black currant syrup. Omit bourbon and fill glass with carbonated water or soda.

Mojito: My friend Wendi and her husband, Murray, enjoyed this drink on vacation in Cuba. Add 2 tsp (10 mL) fresh lime juice to the mint and sugar; stir to dissolve sugar. Use light rum in place of bourbon and fill with soda water.

Herb Mary or Caesar

Herbs add an interesting variation to these tomato-based drinks. They make a tasty beverage to serve at brunch. Serve with a bottle of hot pepper sauce to allow guests to turn up the heat!

3 cups	tomato or tomato-clam juice 750 mL
2 tbsp	finely chopped fresh basil, dill or marjoram (or to taste) 30 mL
1 tbsp	Worcestershire sauce 15 mL
2 tsp	lemon juice 10 mL
1 oz	vodka, optional 30 mL
	Hot pepper sauce, to taste
	Salt and pepper, to taste
	Celery sticks, cherry tomatoes, cooked jumbo shrimp (tails on), for garnish

1. In blender, combine tomato juice, basil, Worcestershire sauce and lemon juice. Purée until well combined.
2. Pour vodka (if using) into a tumbler over ice. Pour tomato-herb mixture into glass; season with hot pepper sauce, salt and pepper.
3. Garnish glass with a celery stick or cherry tomato on a wooden skewer; hook a shrimp or a cherry tomato sliced partway over the rim of the glass.

Makes about 4 servings.

Note

For a Caesar, wipe the outside rim of the glass with a lemon slice, then roll the glass edge in seasoned salt. Fill just below salted edge of rim to prevent salt from getting into the drink.

Index